See Jane
Write

GUNNISON COUNTY LIBRARY DISTRICT
Ann Zugelder Library
307 N. Wisconsin Gunnison, CO 81230
970.641.3485
www.gunnisoncountylibraries.org

See Jane Write

A Girl's Guide to Writing Chick Lit

By Sarah Mlynowski and Farrin Jacobs

QUIRK BOOKS

PHILADELPHIA

Library of Congress Cataloging in Publication Number: 2006900357

ISBN-10: 1-59474-115-8
ISBN-13: 978-1-59474-115-9

Printed in the United States

Typeset in Bulmer, Lucida Sans, and Emmascript

Designed by Susan Van Horn
Illustrations by Chuck Gonzalez

Distributed in North America by Chronicle Books
85 Second Street
San Francisco, CA 94105

10 9 8 7 6 5 4 3 2

Quirk Books
215 Church Street
Philadelphia, PA 19106
www.quirkbooks.com

Contents

Introduction: I Could Write That!

Here's the thing about you: You love chick lit. You read it often, staying loyal to your favorite authors, but you're always willing to open your heart (and eyes) to a new chick on the block. When you read it, you laugh, you smile, you nod your head in recognition, you feel exposed, you feel hopeful. You think, *I've thought that, I've been in that situation, I'm pretty sure I've dated that guy*, and so on, until finally you arrive at, *Hmm, I could write that*.

Here's the thing about us: We're here to tell you, "Yes, you can."

As a bestselling chick lit writer (meet Sarah) and a former chick lit editor (say hello to Farrin), we know a thing or thirty about chick lit. We've watched a lot of good women translate their lives' highs and woes into fiction. And we'd like to share our knowledge with someone who feels she has her own chick lit story locked somewhere inside of her: you.

Despite what you might have heard, there's no formula for chick lit. You can't connect the dots and end up with a bestseller. But you can benefit from advice, and that's what we're here to provide—us and a few of our friends and acquaintances—Meg Cabot, Sarah Dunn, Emily Giffin, Kristin Gore, Marian Keyes, Sophie Kinsella, Nicola Kraus, Emma McLaughlin, and Alisa Valdes-Rodriguez, to name just a few.*

You're probably anxious to get to the guide part of our guide, so

---

*For a full list of the awesome authors who helped us out (and their books), go to page 183.

we'll make this introduction short and sweet. But there are a few things we want to explain about how the book works. It's broken down into two main parts. In part 1, we talk about the general stuff: everything from what exactly chick lit is to how writing chick lit is like dating to how to steamroll your excuses and start your book already. In part 2, we break down the writing process, touching on subjects like choosing your point of view, making your heroine likable, and why you might want to reconsider including a gay best friend in your cast of characters.

We've sprinkled some cheeky but helpful (always helpful!) exercises and sidebars throughout the book. The boxes titled "Mistakes I've Known" let you in on some of Farrin's experiences editing chick lit manuscripts. "It Happened to Me" sidebars offer up anecdotes from Sarah's writing life. "Chick Lit Mad Libs" poke fun at some of the chick lit conventions and highlight the most egregious clichés—so you can avoid them. And "Words of Wisdom," well, that's pretty self-explanatory.

We occasionally take a tough-love approach, but that's because we know you can handle it. You want your novel to be the best it can be. And that's what we want, too.

We hope you enjoy our guide to writing chick lit—and that it helps you become the heroine of your own story.

PART ONE

The Big Picture

ONE
What Exactly Is Chick Lit?

✳ ✳ ✳

Contrary to popular belief, chick lit is not all about shoes. Or clothes. Or purses. Yes, some chick lit characters enjoy their fashion collections, but if an interest in designer names is what made you pick up this book, maybe you should grab *Vogue* instead. Chick lit is also not all about getting a guy. Love may be a happy diversion, or a painful pothole, but the chick lit story is about the main character's road to self-discovery. Although there's usually a satisfying and uplifting conclusion, the ending is more about hope for the future than snagging Mr. Right.

So if it's not about shoes and guys, then what exactly is it? Well, chick lit is often upbeat, always funny fiction about contemporary female characters and their everyday struggles with work, home, friendship, family, or love. It's about women growing up and figuring out who they are and what they need versus what they think they want. It's about observing life and finding the humor in a variety of situations, exchanges, and people. It's about coming of age (no matter how old the woman is—chick lit heroines can be anywhere from teenaged to beyond middle-aged). It's generally written by women for women. It's honest, it reflects women's lives today—their hopes and dreams as well as their trials and tribulations—and, well, it's hugely popular.

But you already knew all that, right? (Just nod your head and make us happy.)

A Brief History of Chick Lit

When Bridget Jones hopped the pond and sailed into U.S. book-stores in 1998, she changed the world of women's fiction forever. Helen Fielding wasn't necessarily the first chick lit author, but with *Bridget Jones's Diary*, she was certainly the most popular. And her timing, as Bridget might say, was v. good. Girl-centric television shows like *Ally McBeal* and *Sex and the City* were making waves, landing on the covers of mainstream magazines and gaining fans at a rapid pace. Clearly, women were ready for these types of characters and the stories of their lives and loves. Alongside Bridget sat Laura Zigman's *Animal Husbandry*, followed by Suzanne Finnamore's *Otherwise Engaged* and Melissa Bank's *The Girls' Guide to Hunting and Fishing*, and with their success, publishers knew a bona fide trend was in the making.

No longer were the ladies at the center of popular women's nov-els limited to windblown tragic heroines (care of Danielle Steele) or descendents of Hollywood/mob dynasties (thank you, Jackie Collins)—the kinds of characters who populated the bestseller lists in the 1980s and '90s. Now they were the girls next door. These young women had been around in contemporary fiction (check out Rona Jaffe's *The Best of Everything* and Gail Parent's *Sheila Levine Is Dead and Living in New York* for some pre–chick lit chick lit), but they had never made their mark on publishing in quite this lucrative way.

Of course, there was Jane Austen, surely the mother of all chick lit, but in popular contemporary fiction this was something new. And publishers were taking note. Soon they began marketing more books as chick lit (which they quickly decided meant pastel covers and shoes).

These days, you can't walk into a bookstore without spotting at least a couple, but most likely more, chick lit novels on the New Fiction display, and some stores even have tables or shelves reserved solely for the ladies in pink.

Which is lucky for you, since you're interested in writing chick lit and all.

THE MAKING OF MODERN CHICK LIT

1995: Marian Keyes publishes her first novel, *Watermelon*, in Ireland.

1996: Along comes Bridget Jones in the UK and the dawn of the chick lit craze.

1998: *Bridget Jones's Diary, Animal Husbandry,* and *The Girls' Guide to Hunting and Fishing* are published in the United States.

2000–2001: American publishers continue to dip their toes into the chick lit pond with titles such as Valerie Frankel's *Smart vs. Pretty,* Jennifer Weiner's *Good in Bed,* and British imports *Jemima J,* by Jane Green, *Getting Over It,* by Anna Maxted, and *Confessions of a Shopaholic,* by Sophie Kinsella.

2001: Harlequin Enterprises is among the first to capitalize on the trend with a dedicated chick lit imprint, launching Red Dress Ink with Melissa Senate's *See Jane Date*. Other publishers, such as Simon & Schuster (Downtown Press) and Kensington (Strapless), follow shortly afterward.

2005: Warner Books launches the imprint 5 Spot, confirming that chick lit is here to stay.

"It's Only Chick Lit"

The chick lit label can be a mixed blessing. Without it, a lot of your favorite books might never have seen the light of day. But because of it, some of those same titles get no respect. "I think *chick lit* has become a negative term, and it's one that's used primarily as a way to put female writers in their place," says Sarah Dunn, *New York Times* bestselling author of *The Big Love*. "On the other hand, as a publishing trend it has been positive for a lot of women, some of whom wouldn't have gotten their novels published at all if the chick lit thing hadn't taken off the way it did. But if you live by the sword, you die by it too."

Caren Lissner, whose first novel, *Carrie Pilby*, had been making the publishing rounds and getting good feedback for a while before an editor at a designated chick lit imprint took a chance on it,* sees it in a stark business sense: "It's a marketing term, and I am grateful for anything that helped get my books into the hands of readers."

The problem with the term is that many (misguided) people automatically assume that chick lit means a tale about a twenty-

---

I was that editor!—FJ

something trying to find love in the big city. While that may have been true once, these days chick lit casts a wide net: Stories can be about anything from dating to dealing with death. Walk into your local bookstore and take a look at how diverse the novels have become.

Of course, people love to label, and chick lit has already been divided into many subgenres. There are those based on the supposed life stages of the heroine: Teen Lit (girl juggling her issues at home and at school); Single-in-the-City Lit (young woman living in New York/London gets dumped and tries to find her way in the urban jungle); Bride Lit (young woman about to walk down the aisle, or walking behind her friend down the aisle); Mom Lit (young woman juggling life, kids, and desires); and even Hen Lit (young-at-heart woman juggling life, kids, desires, and grandkids).

Then there's chick lit cross-pollinated with other genres: Mystery Chick Lit (hip woman solving crimes); Christian Lit (not only is she trying to find a man—she's trying to find God); Multicultural Lit (everyday struggles with an ethnic slant); and Paranormal Lit (everyday struggles—except the protagonist happens to be vampire/witch).

There are also thematic subgenres: Gossip Lit (she knows the goods); Assistant Lit (she works for the woman who knows the goods); Plus-Sized Lit (she's no size four) . . .

Basically, if you write it in a cheeky tone and a publisher slaps a clever title and a cute cover on it, people will call your novel chick lit. There are worse things your novel could be called.

Critics and even other female writers (ones who fancy themselves serious, literary novelists) tend to treat chick lit as some subpar version of Real Writing. Don't listen to them. As with any other type of book out there, there's bad chick lit and good chick lit. Books filled with cardboard characters and cardboard writing are published nearly as often as (if not more than) those brought to life by unique voices and endearing protagonists. Some trip from one cliché to another, while others offer twists and turns that feel wholly original. We want you to write good chick lit. That's why we're here.

Chick Lit Is Dead; Long Live Chick Lit

Don't worry; despite the death knell people have been sounding for chick lit for years, it's not going anywhere. Readers continue to flock to it, and the books continue to fly off the shelves in all their versatile glory. The fact that there are so many types of chick lit available helps propel the market forward and ensures that it will continue to thrive. It's a genre that will evolve with the times to give women fiction that is relevant to their lives. And although one BBC critic attacked chick lit by claiming the novels "merely hold a mirror up to women's lives," we say, "Yeah, so what?"

Sometimes looking in the mirror is a valuable way to learn and grow. Because chick lit is like life . . . but funnier. When you peer into the reflection, maybe you learn something by example, maybe you don't, but we guarantee that you'll be entertained. It's true that publishers who once saturated the market are now determined to publish only the best of the best. But as long as people still enjoy reading chick lit, the books will keep coming.

Maybe one with your name on it.

Two

Getting Back at Your Ex and Other Reasons to Write

* * *

Something is compelling you to write your own chick lit novel. Do you know what it is? People sit down and morph into writers for any number of reasons—personal, professional, and financial. Want to know why and how a few published authors took their first steps toward chick lit? Let's start off with a personal story.

How Sarah Became a Chick Lit Author*

The first novel I wrote was called *Lizzie Forshort* and was about a girl named Elizabeth (Lizzie for short—get it?) who moves to a new city with her parents, makes new friends, and wins the lottery. I thought it up during writing time in third grade and scrawled three atrociously spelled words per line until I wrote "The End." My mom edited it, typed it up, and sent it to Bantam Books. Not surprisingly, this is also the story of my very first rejection letter. I vowed that one day I would get an acceptance letter. (I didn't realize then that when a novel is accepted, there's a phone call, no letter.)

I kept writing throughout high school and college (including a column for the school paper called the S-Files, which ruminated on important subjects such as the sociological implications of the end of *Seinfeld*, and how to get frat boys to buy you drinks), but decided I would put off working on novels until much later. Who was going to take a twenty-two-year-old novelist seriously? And anyway, I needed a job. Badly.

I got hired in the marketing department at Harlequin Enterprises—the romance publisher. My job involved working with books such as (I kid you not) *The Virgin Bride Said, "Wow!," The Texas Sheik's Runaway Princess*, and *The Millionaire Cowboy*. My personal life, on the other hand, was wedding- and millionaire-free. I shared a small mouse-infested apartment with a neat-freak roommate, my boyfriend had just broken up with me and booked a monthlong trip to Australia, and I had somehow accumulated a five-thousand-dollar credit card debt (Canadian dollars, but still). The irony of my situation wasn't lost on me.

In my very own words.—SM

When I wasn't at work or on the town, I was reading. Free from *Beowulf*, *Ulysses*, and other sleep-inducing university classics, I suddenly had time for pleasure reading again, and like every other gen-X or gen-Y woman, I discovered *Bridget Jones's Diary*. As Bridget navigated her way through London's nightlife, her dead-end career, and dating Mr. Wrong, I couldn't stop laughing. I then lost myself in the bookstore and devoured every piece of British chick lit I could find.

At about the same time (early 2000), the word on the Harlequin grapevine was that they were planning to launch a new line of single-in-the-city books. I heard the marketing person talking about it in the bathroom. "I love the concept," she said while applying her lipstick. "But where are we going to find the writers?"

Interesting, I thought. Where could they find a twenty-something wannabe novelist who could write about bad boyfriends who ditch you and roommates who eat all your Chinese food?

I prophesized the future: What if I became a published author? My ex would finally appreciate how fabulous I am! Of course, by the time he realized it, I would be far too glamorous to date him, and he would be forever kicking himself about how he lost the best thing that ever happened to him. Sucker. Plus, I could pay off my credit card . . .

I wrote the opening line of *Milkrun*: "Jerk. Jerk, jerk, jerk. I can't believe what a complete jerk he is." When I finished the book, Harlequin bought it. They paid me seven thousand (American!) dollars. Not only did I pay off my credit card debt, I treated myself to two new pairs of shoes.

How They Became Chick Lit Authors

And here's how some of your favorite chick lit authors got started:

Caren Lissner began working on *Carrie Pilby* when she got the idea for a character who was book smart but people dumb. Jennifer Weiner wrote *Good in Bed* in the aftermath of a breakup. "I wanted to tell the story of a girl who was a lot like me; a guy who was a lot like Satan, and give the girl a happy ending," she writes on her Web site. Jennifer O'Connell had been attending a writing workshop for three months before she got the idea for her debut novel, *Bachelorette #1*. Kristin Gore worked in television before she took the plunge and wrote *Sammy's Hill*. "Though I enjoyed the energy and collaboration of TV work," she says, "I longed to develop my own stories and characters, and in a more in-depth way. In my own life, I don't watch very much television, but I constantly read books. I decided to risk doing something that was more intrinsically *me*."

International bestsellers Sophie Kinsella and Marian Keyes both started out of an urge to write something they'd want to read. "I wanted to write a full-blown comedy," says Kinsella, who'd already published dark comedies under her real name. "But really, the prompt was having the idea for a shopaholic character!"* Keyes felt there were no books at the time about ordinary women. "There were wish-fulfillment books about rich people, but I wanted something which explained and explored the postfeminist real world, so

---

*Fun Tidbit: *Sophie Kinsella submitted* Confessions of a Shopaholic *anonymously. "I was already published under my real name, Madeleine Wickham, and the first* Shopaholic *book was kind of a secret experiment. I wanted it to be judged on its own merit, so I sent it to my publishers under my pen name, Sophie Kinsella. Only one person knew the truth. When they made an offer, I felt like it was my first book deal all over again!"*

I decided to write one."

Your Turn!

Now that you know the story of some of chick lit royalty's humble beginnings, what will yours be? You're a blank page, so at this point, anything goes. The important thing is to keep your expectations in check.

Take our true or false quiz to see if any of these reasons apply to you.

YOU WANT TO WRITE A CHICK LIT BOOK BECAUSE . . .

1. Your ex will be browsing in a bookstore when he'll spot a glamorous photo poster announcing your upcoming sure-to-be-packed signing. He will immediately feel like a moron for breaking your heart and show up at the event in an attempt to win you back. Unfortunately for your ex, your handsome, sensitive, mogul husband is by your side. (Feel free to replace ex-boyfriend with ex-friend/former boss/father-who-deserted-your-family-for-a-slut-of-a-secretary-when-you-were-ten. Basically anyone who's pissed you off.)
   ☐ True   ☐ False

2. After you've devoted ten years of your life to him, your beloved cat just went gently into the night. You feel writing about your sadness will help you deal with it. (The first part of the sentence can be replaced by any action, *beloved cat* by any noun, and *went gently into the night* can be, well, anything that caused you pain.

Such as "After *you accidentally left the stove on*, your *townhouse just burned down.*)"

☐ True   ☐ False

3. You're broke. Writers make good money, right?

☐ True   ☐ False

4. You fantasize about quitting your crappy day job. The day after you sell your book, you'll call up your boss and tell her you're not coming in. "Today?" she'll ask. "Ever," you'll chirp. You can already picture yourself working in your fluffy orange sweatpants.

☐ True   ☐ False

5. You were made for a life of glamour. Move over Sykes sisters. You will go on tour in New York! London! Milan! You will drink Bellinis and cartwheel right over those velvet ropes. You're ready for the A-list, baby.

☐ True   ☐ False

6. You're kind of lonely and you'd like some attention. Specifically, you never had a pen pal growing up and could use some fan mail.

☐ True   ☐ False

Oh, not me, you scream. I want to write purely because of my love of the written word!

Liar, liar, pants on fire.

It's OK to answer *true* and admit that one of these reasons is (partially) driving you to write. But we hope that at least part of your motivation to write a chick lit novel is that you have a story to tell and you think people will enjoy reading it.

You don't have to be ashamed of your less-than-altruistic motives, since they are most likely what will drive you to obtain your goal. Just try to keep your expectations realistic.

If you answered true to number one: You want to get back at your ex. Show the world what a jerk he was. Or maybe your parents made you the rope in their tug-of-war, and you want them to finally see how much damage they've done. That's fine. Healthy even. Just remember that libel = lawsuit. And that writing a book (it's a *lot* of work, after all) should be about more than revenge. Besides, what happens when you "make up" with the person you bitch-slapped? You know how family members like to dredge up that awful thing you said at every possible opportunity? Now imagine what happens when that awful thing you said is in print. Available in bookstores. Forever.

Ideally, the best thing you can take from your breakup/hurt is the drive to improve your life. Because we all know (warning: cliché ahead) that *living well is the best revenge.*

It Happened to Me

Remember the ex who inspired *Milkrun*? And the opening, "Jerk. Jerk, jerk jerk"? Well, see, we kind of ended up getting back together a few months before the book came out, and then we kind of got married. And *every single* wedding speech started with the quote, "Jerk, jerk, jerk."—SM

Number two: Writing through your pain. Totally valid. That's why we have a chapter about how writing chick lit is like therapy.

And about numbers three, four, and five: You're broke, you want to quit your day job, and you want to be famous—ha! This is not a get-rich-quick book. Unfortunately, writing a chick lit novel is not going to instantly solve your problems. Even if you start writing today, at the *earliest*, you won't see a dollar for at least a year and a half. In the best-case scenario, think six to nine months to write your book, three to six months to find an agent, three months to find a publisher, three months to sign the contracts, another month to receive the check. And sorry to burst your bubble, but that first check will be small, so you'll have to wait at least another year for the book to go on sale, and then another year to earn any royalties (more about the numbers in chapter 13).

This is not to say that you will never get rich writing chick lit. There are several authors swimming in money. Yes, you should aim high, but we're being realistic here. And it's unlikely that you're going to get rich after one book.

So, if it's going to take a while to make money—and unless you have a wealthy husband/mom/dad/generous friend or are willing to drastically change your lifestyle—you can't just quit your day job.

Most chick lit authors publish at least two novels before they leave their jobs. And others are still doing double duty. Which causes a bit of a catch-22: If you hate your day job, but have to keep it until you're settled in your writing, how are you ever going to find the time to go to work and then write on top of that? You have to be disciplined, that's how. (See chapter 5 for some hints.) And you have to keep your eye on the prize—your completed novel. Don't just whine about hating your job—let your dissatisfaction at work inspire you to write.

> "Like Rachel in *Something Borrowed*, I loved law school, but I didn't enjoy being an attorney at a big corporate firm. The culture was stifling and the hours demanding. I discovered that there's nothing like a little misery to motivate you to make a change."—Emily Giffin, *New York Times* bestselling author of *Something Borrowed*

On the plus side, if you make it over all the hurdles, once you establish your career and decide that you want to work from home, yes, you *can* work in your pajamas. Your fans will never know. In fact, they'll encourage it. In writing. Because if you publish a chick lit novel (and let readers know where they can reach you via a Web site or e-mail address), we guarantee you will get some fan mail. Readers are friendly and supportive and love to tell writers what they think.*

Except for the readers who are unfriendly and opinionated but also love to tell writers what they think.

One More Reason: You Love Chick Lit

Take Ethel. She studied English lit and reads a book a month (mostly mysteries). She's always wanted to be a novelist but never knew what to write. And then she read all those articles in the paper about chick lit and spotted all the pink shoe-y books on the best-seller lists, and thought, *That's what I should write!* Fine, she's not a fan of those girly books, but *how hard can it be?* Dumped girl + assistant job in publishing + gay best friend = let the fun begin!

See Ethel struggling through her first draft. See Ethel sending her manuscripts out to agents and publishers. See Ethel opening her rejection letters. Why? Well, writing good chick lit is not just hard. It's *really* hard—especially when you're not a chick lit fan. It's tough enough to write an entire novel as it is, never mind in a voice that doesn't come naturally to you. Agents, editors, and readers can sniff out a nonauthentic voice from miles away.

Ethel should sit down and think about the type of book that speaks to her, that she loves, that she can't put down. And write one of those.

Now back to you. Let's say you love chick lit. You consider Cannie, Bridget, and Nanny your soul sisters. The first time you cracked the spine on a shoe-clad book, you screamed, *Omigod, I want to write something like this!*

You, on the other hand, can make it happen. You know your target audience: *you.*

So now you're ready to try your hand at it. Remember, the biggest thing that separates you from the authors you've read is that they've sat down and written a book, and you haven't. But other than that being-published thing, they're just like you. They even read chick lit.

And while we more than support everyone's chick lit habit (especially if you have already bought or plan to buy the collected works of Sarah Mlynowski), please, please, please, make sure not to limit your reading to *only* chick lit. While you're coming up with your story idea, it might be helpful to read other types of books, too. Read the classics, the contemporary classics, bestselling books, cult favorites, books by men, short story collections, memoirs . . . whatever you can get your hands on that might interest you. Alisa Valdes-Rodriguez was inspired by chick lit writer Terry McMillan. But she also reads a lot of Dean Koontz. "Any and everything of his," she admits. "He's a master of plot and timing. . . . I love that he can take a formula and, while working within its confines, create works of startling creativity."

It Happened to Me

I got the idea for *Fishbowl* after reading *The Poisonwood Bible.* Yes, I know that Christian missionaries in Africa don't seem to inspire the story of three roommates who accidentally burn down their apartment, but it was the alternating voices that did it for me. I had never seen it done before, and I thought it was a brilliant technique. I thought the she said/she said/she said roommate points of view would be fun to write and read.—*SM*

On the other hand, let's say you don't read chick lit. You read Jonathan Franzen and Margaret Atwood and Zadie Smith and Don DeLillo. But there's a story about a twenty-something woman editor/lawyer/astronaut that's been growing inside you since you were ten, and it's dying to get out. And it's going to be funny and upbeat, and . . . is it chick lit? Maybe. But instead of worrying about labels, *focus on writing your book*. When Emily Giffin was working on her first book, she had no idea that she was writing chick lit. "I don't think I really believed that my novel would one day be published, so I wasn't thinking in terms of genre or marketing or sparkly diamond rings adorning pretty, pink book jackets. I was simply telling a story about a woman who fell in love with her best friend's fiancé—a story about love and friendship and how complicated both can be." Focus on finishing the story you want to tell, not on what people will call it once it's done.

Where Do Chick Lit Writers Come From?

No, you don't need a master's in creative writing. It doesn't matter what you studied. Really. What all writers have in common is that they read. A lot.

They also write a lot. Maybe they keep diaries, or blogs, or have hundreds of short stories on their computers. Or maybe they're professionals. If you're already a journalist or a scriptwriter, then you probably feel pretty comfortable making the jump. Kristin Gore benefited from her pre-chick lit career as a TV comedy writer. "I learned to meet deadlines, collaborate, rewrite ad infinitum, laugh at myself and others, and not take anything too seriously."

But writing novels is different from any other type of professional writing. After making the switch, Gore realized that she'd have to make some other changes, too. "I no longer had the immediate quality checks that come with working with a group of hilarious, brutally honest people," she says. "I had to learn to live with the perpetual fear that I might be the only one who would ever think that what I was writing was funny or good. I had to learn to trust myself more. I also had to remember to make an effort to interact with other humans, since it turns out I make an excellent recluse." Laura Caldwell needed to lose most of her lawyer speak. "I had to unlearn formality in writing. The first draft of *Burning the Map* was littered with phrases like, 'hereintofor after referred to as . . .'"

Basically, any education and experience you have will help you with your writing. Think about *The Nanny Diaries*, *The Devil Wears Prada*, *Good in Bed*, and *Milkrun*. The protagonist's job in each of them is loosely (or not so loosely) based on a job the author had. Knowledge about an industry will only help ground your character. You studied biology? Excellent. We bet you could come up with metaphors that we never would have.

Laura Caldwell definitely appreciates her training. "I thank the vocational gods that I went to law school. The schooling and the corporate environment gave me lots of material." The fact that she can comfortably set her books in the world of law without much research is a major advantage over those who've, say, only worked in publishing. And it's not just about the material. The skills Caldwell picked up on the job were even more useful. "The practice of law, the dreaded daily billing, gave me an immense amount of discipline, for which I'm always grateful."

Alison Pace, author of *If Andy Warhol Had a Girlfriend*, acknowledges that her research job at an art gallery helped her in a variety of ways. "I learned a lot about working on my own and setting deadlines for myself." She was also able to write a story about the art world, an original setting for a chick lit novel. "There is so much information in there that I never would have had, had I not spent a decade working in that world," she says.

So you've always wanted to write, but instead of studying literature you took astrophysics and spent two years working for NASA? Trust us: Write what you know. We can already see the moonboots on the cover.

THREE

How Writing Chick Lit Is Like Therapy

* * *

So you've decided now is the time—you're ready to tackle your chick lit novel. But before you start, you have some work to do, and we're not talking about deciding what to name your characters or making sure your printer is stocked with paper. (Besides, printer paper? That's what your day job is for, silly!) No, the kind of work we're talking about involves something a little more personal: examining yourself.

A common problem in chick lit manuscripts is that the writer is entrenched in her own worldview. Of course, we support writing what you know, but you have to truly understand what that is. If you're not open to analyzing the world around you and your point of view, your story and characters will lack dimension and your book will fall flat. In order to create a believable fictional world, you might need to do some personal homework about the situations and characters you want to write about. Sure, chick lit is about having fun, but in order to allow your reader to have that good time, you need to have a little lie-down on the couch.

Session One: Why Am I Here?

If you've ever been to therapy (it's OK, you can admit it, we're all friends here), you know that one of the first questions the good doctor will ask is some form of "So, what brings you here?" Sometimes the answer is simple—a difficult breakup, a death in the family, body-image issues—and sometimes it's not, and therapy itself will help you find that answer. Think about why you've picked up this book, why you want to write chick lit. (Blaming your parents is completely allowed; just remember to thank them in your acknowledgments.) As with real therapy, your catalyst might be right in front of you, or you may have to dig a little deeper to break down a complex reason. Be sure not to hold back here—no reason is unreasonable. If it's revenge that has brought you to the computer, there ain't no shame in that. It's just important that you know the feeling exists.

Stacey Ballis, author of *Inappropriate Men*, says that sometimes the writing process helps her see things in a new light. "When my characters go to dark places, which everyone has to do at one point or another, my own experiences certainly play into it. And I think drawing on my life in that way, with an attempt at objectivity, can bring some clarity about myself and my actions."

It wasn't until after Johanna Edwards's *The Next Big Thing* was published that she addressed one of her issues head-on. "My writing has made me a lot more self-confident," she says. "I've always been a shy, somewhat insecure person. Through my novels I've been able to communicate a lot of my insecurities, and many women have approached me and told me they struggle with the same self-esteem issues and insecurities that I do. It's been so liberating! I truly realized I'm not the only person who feels dorky or awkward or shy from time to time. And it's made me so much more outgoing and confident."

Of course, for some writers, a chick lit book is just a chick lit book. They get an idea and they run with it. Or they start to build a story in their mind, and they can't stop. But chances are there is some theme or story line that is ripped from the headlines of their lives in one way or another.

For Valerie Frankel, it wasn't so much that she started to write out of a certain feeling as it was that she started to write to end that feeling. "I began working on *The Accidental Virgin* after my first husband died, and that book provided a much-needed distraction during that horrible time," she says. "The simple act of plotting and thinking and typing helped me get through it—not the content of the book itself. But writing definitely helped. More than I thought it would."

Words of Wisdom

"I can assure you that you will never finish any piece of writing if you don't understand what motivates you to write in the first place and if you don't honor that impulse, whether it's exile or assimilation, redemption or destruction, revenge or love."
—*The Forest for the Trees*, by Betsy Lerner

Session Two: Who or What Am I Writing About?

Once you've figured out the why, the who/what should be no problem. But make sure you're looking at your designated characters or scenario from all sides. Say yours is an idea fueled by a recent breakup. You're still so angry you refer to your ex merely as That Jackass I Used to Date, and you've concocted a story that will paint him in the worst light possible. Before you write a whole novel filled with tales of That Jackass (let's call him that for short, OK?), focus on a few reasons why you liked him in the first place. It might be hard, but surely there was *something* that drew you to him when he still deserved to be called by his given name. You did go out with him, after all. (But don't go falling in love with him again, and *definitely* don't call him and tell him you were just thinking about him.)

IT WASN'T ALL BAD . . .

MAKING THE WHO/WHAT BELIEVABLE

1. At the top of a piece of paper, write down the name of the person or a brief description of the situation you're writing about.

2. Now draw a line down the middle of the page, and on one side write down everything positive about that person or situation.

3. On the other side of the sheet, get down every negative quality. It's OK if one side outweighs the other, just make sure you have at least one entry in each column.

4. Apply the same technique to ex-boyfriends, stepmothers, run-down apartments, bad jobs, and so on. In the end, you'll have the tools to make your narrative real and your characters believable rather than one-dimensional.

Why, you might be asking, should he get any good press in your book? Because if you depict him as evil incarnate, (a) you're making it impossible for your reader to understand what your jilted narrator saw in him in the first place, and (b) you're painting your narrator as a girl with some seriously bad taste in people, which makes her a little less sympathetic.

Of course, don't go making That Jackass a saint. Just be sure that somewhere he gets to be charming or smart or good in bed, even if it's just in a flashback. Your reader needs to believe that these characters connected on some level, at some point, about something. And as an added bonus, thinking about That Jackass in this way just might help you add depth to your characterization and dimension to your story line. Also, it might curb that urge to TP his house. (For more on making your characters realistic, check out chapter 7, "Your Friends and Neighbors.")

Session Three: Let It All Out

You've got a lot going on in that pretty little head of yours, and now is your chance to let it all out. Think of the writing process as a way to right some wrongs, undo what's been done, or do what was left undone. It's your opportunity to vent, reveal, create, and release.

Robyn Harding found certain aspects of writing *The Journal of Mortifying Moments* both cathartic and enlightening because she was able to give her character wisdom and strength that she'd lacked in a particular circumstance. "Years ago, I had a relationship similar to the one between Kerry and gorgeous Sam. I felt, as Kerry's mom says, 'he was the best I could do,' and therefore put up with all sorts of crappy treatment. I also stayed with him because I was worried about what other people would think if I ended it (I had a rather rocky relationship history). He finally dumped me. I wish I'd had the courage to say, 'This relationship is a train wreck,' and to leave him months earlier. I didn't. But I did give Kerry the guts to break off her engagement to gorgeous Sam, which felt really good."

Stacey Ballis also likes to get some satisfaction through her fiction: "I will re-create discussions where my characters get to say the stuff I only thought of in the car after the real conversation was over." If only we could do that in real life.

Session Four: Enough About Me, What Do You Think About Me?

Yes, yes, we know you're smart and funny and talented (we definitely know you have good taste in how-to books), but in order to project the most appealing parts of you onto one of your characters, you need to try to see yourself as others do. This might involve talking to your friends about certain qualities you want to play up in your characters or just paying close attention to how people react to you in different situations. You might see yourself as shy, for example, but others might perceive your behavior as bitchy. (Of course, we're just assuming that if this is your first novel, the protagonist is some version of you, for better or for worse. We could totally be wrong, though, and if we are, we're deeply sorry. We offer up more specifics on creating your main character in chapter 6.)

Words of Wisdom

"You are going to love some of your characters, because they are you or some facet of you, and you are going to hate some of your characters for the same reason."—*Bird by Bird*, by Anne Lamott

Just as a therapist might tell you things you don't want to hear or lead you to self-discoveries you'd have preferred remain in that happy place called denial, when you're writing a character in your own image (yes, you're pretty much the god of your fictional universe, so let there be light), you might have to analyze some flaws or unsavory behaviors you've always preferred to ignore or maybe even were completely unaware of. But it's OK. Because (a) nobody's perfect, (b) a character's flaws are often what make her even more endearing, and (c) you're human, and if you want to, you can learn from your mistakes.

Session Five: The Way I See It

Consider what you like about your favorite books. Beyond the writing and the plot, what a lot of people respond to in a novel is how the main character sees the world. You can relate to her thoughts and actions. You can see yourself in her shoes (and carrying her knock-off Prada purse). You find the things she says to be funny or true or off-the-wall but totally logical. What this means is the author has done a good job of creating someone who feels whole and real—and she's done this by being able to see beyond her own nose. In order to create the same effect in your novel, make sure that you understand enough about the situations and people you're writing about to craft believable scenarios no matter how your reader looks at it. If, for example, the idea for your story is based on a theory you have about men and women, test that theory out on some friends to make sure it's something others can relate to. If no one can understand the way your characters see the world, you'll have a hard time getting people interested in reading about them.

Session Six: It's All Relative

Sometimes therapy is about logic and common sense, so with that in mind, let's just state the obvious: Characters need to relate to each other. You can have the greatest plot in the world, but unless your characters connect in a believable way, that plot might as well be a hole in the ground.

Consider your own relationships: Who are your friends? How did you meet them and what keeps them in your life? Think about the dynamics of how you interact. Do you have one friend who never leaves enough money when you're paying the tab? Have you ever thought about why? Sure, maybe she's just a cheapskate. But consider this: Maybe she's bad at math and would be horrified to know that she's been cheating you for years. If you were to write about her, you'd want to try to see the world through her eyes. When you're creating your characters, being open to other points of view and getting into the head of the people you're bringing to life will help create believable relationship dynamics.

You should also be sure that everyone's in your novel for a reason that makes sense within the world of the story. Don't just put people together without knowing who they are and how they might react to each other. It's fine to put in someone for comic relief, but make sure that's not the only purpose the character serves. The bottom line is this: Know your characters, know why they're there, and you will be rewarded with fictional people who can relate to each other in a real way. Meanwhile, your reader will be rewarded with characters she'll want to follow from beginning to "The End." (We'll delve deeper into this secondary character stuff in chapter 7.)

And that's all the time we have for today. We'll be billing your health insurance.

FOUR

How Writing Chick Lit Is Like Dating

✳ ✳ ✳

Think about it: What do you want to achieve with your novel (besides fame, fortune, and an addiction to checking your sales ranking on Amazon.com)? You want to charm your reader. You want to put your best face forward. You want to be lovable and entertaining, but you also want to be taken seriously. Basically, writing chick lit is like dating. So before you sit down to write, peruse our rules. (If it's like dating, then there must be rules, right?) Who knows—while helping you turn your great idea into a fantastic chick lit novel, we might just help you turn your next date into a spectacular one.

Rule #1: Be true to yourself.

If you pretend to be someone you're not, your writing voice will sound forced. And if you pretend to be someone you're not on a date, (a) your date will see right through you, (b) you'll end up dating someone who's all wrong for you (statements like "I love playing ice hockey, too!" have rarely led to anything but trouble), or (c) eventually you'll have to come clean because you can't fake your way through an entire relationship (well, you can, but you might not respect yourself in the morning).

Aspiring chick lit authors can end up writing someone else's book instead of their own. They think that in order to be successful, their narrator should speak a certain way, have a specific job, wear a particular brand of shoes. But if the world they've created isn't one they understand or would gravitate toward naturally, the reader will be able to tell. That doesn't mean you have to be a twenty-two-year-old virgin in order to write from the point of view of a twenty-two-year-old virgin—this is fiction, after all—but if you have no clue about what drives your character, what thoughts go through her mind, then she won't come off sounding true.

Mistakes I've Known

I've gotten tons of manuscripts from older women trying to sound like twenty-five-year-old hipsters, recent college grads trying to affect the voice of a hardened career girl, and women who've never spent a day in New York City trying to work the attitude of a grizzled Manhattanite. Sure, some people can pull off these hat tricks, but I'm here to tell you that most can't. When one page of dialogue is peppered with multiple *hotties*,

hey, girlfriends, or references to that *hunkola's buns*, I know I'm
reading a faker.—*FJ*

Also, don't try to write a book because you think that's what's
going to sell. In addition to not being true to yourself, you might be
shooting yourself in the foot. Who's to say what's hot now will be
hot by the time you finish your book?

Rule #2: Always have your wit about you.

Sense of humor is key—in chick lit and in the wonderful world of
dating. We're not saying you have to be a comedian and that you
need to generate a laugh a minute, but if you've got no funny in you,
you might want to reconsider this whole thing. The most important
part of using humor to your advantage is you have to have a sense of
humor about yourself. Same goes for a date: If you take yourself too
seriously, you just might be taking yourself out of the game. Dating
should be fun (when it's not torture or, at best, mind-bendingly awkward), and so should the chick lit experience.

That doesn't mean you can't tackle serious subjects. Lolly
Winston's *Good Grief* is a perfect example. Take the opening passage:

> How can I be a widow? Widows wear horn-
> rimmed glasses and cardigan sweaters that smell
> like mothballs and have crepe-paper skin and
> names like Gladys or Midge and meet with their
> other widow friends once a week to play pinochle.

The subject matter is huge and serious: the death of her narrator's husband. But what makes the novel so successful is the way the narrator looks at the world. If she'd opened with "Why me? Why is the world so random and cruel?" it's not likely *Good Grief* would've been firmly planted on the bestseller lists. Winston's character suffered, but it was never a chore to read about it.

Rule #3: There's a fine line between clever and catty.

Making fun of a bitchy colleague—fine. Making fun of the nice girl in the office because she's painfully shy and hasn't had a date this millennium—not fine. So much of chick lit is centered around revenge and spite, but you have to earn that for your character. Likewise, if you go on a date and spend ten minutes taking potshots (however clever they may be) at the flustered waitress, your date is not walking away with a warm fuzzy feeling.

Writing a character who's more nasty than you realize happens to the best of us. Meg Cabot, bestselling author of *The Boy Next Door*, admits that she had this problem with the first "chick litty book" she ever wrote. "I didn't realize it until I gave the manuscript to friends to read, and they were like, 'This girl sucks.' I was mortified," she says. "I put the manuscript away and read it months later and realized they were right. I had to do some major revisions. I've only just sold this particular book, though I've published four other adult chick lits in the meantime. It's still being revised, but I think I've got it down now. I definitely learned my lesson, and fast."

Words of Wisdom

"Continuous immersion in the mind of a wholly unsympathetic character would be intolerable for both writer and reader."

—*The Art of Fiction*, by David Lodge

Rule #4: Just because it looks easy doesn't mean it is.

You've heard it a million times from Oprah—relationships take work. So does writing chick lit. Sure, it looks easy—after all, chick lit is cute, has a handle on pop culture, makes you laugh, will spend Sunday mornings in bed with you, and was totally trying to look down your shirt—but if you're really in it for the long haul (that is, if you want to finish your novel), you've got to be willing to put your heart into it. Whether it's making compromises (watch TV or work on your novel?) or doing some despised legwork, in this relationship, you've got to be willing to take one for the team.

Carole Matthews (*With or Without You*) admits to expecting her first novel to be one big honeymoon after the first short story she ever wrote won a national competition. "I confess that I then thought, 'How hard can it be?' But as soon as I tried to write a novel, I realized that it was never going to be a walk in the park!"

Rule #5: It should feel right.

Have you ever continued to date someone long after you determined he wasn't the one for you? You know the feelings—everything he says, does, thinks begins to annoy you. Suddenly you find yourself disgusted by the way he breathes. Or maybe yours is the guy who is just not cool to you—after you spend time with him you feel like crap about yourself, your friends despise him, he's mean to old ladies and small animals. And yet . . . you hold on. *Don't do that.* And don't keep working on a story or with a character you hate writing. Now, we're not saying that every time you hit a rough patch you should give up. Au contraire—you need to write through that. But if every time you think about sitting down to write, you are filled with dread, well, it's possible that, to borrow a phrase, you're just not that into your book.

Meg Cabot (who also happens to be the gazillion-selling author of *The Princess Diaries*) found herself getting that not-so-right feeling when she tried working on a book from the male point of view. "So," she says simply, "I decided that writing from a guy's perspective isn't for me." And you know what? She's done all right for herself anyway.

Rule #6: Just because you're the only girl at the table doesn't mean you're the only person in the world.

Remember the rule about catty versus clever? The same holds true for self-absorbed and self-aware. On a date, this means if you've been talking for an hour straight, you might want to take a breather, maybe ask that guy you've been talking at a question or three. In your writing, this means you need to let your character interact with people rather than simply have people revolve around her. Your girl—of course she's the A plot. But the B plot needs its time in the spotlight, too.

Rule #7: Don't be afraid of commitment.

We know, we've come of age in a time of choice. We're overloaded with options, overburdened by the weight of decision making, but for the love of Jane Austen, just commit to an idea and start writing. It's fine to play around with a few different ideas until one emerges as the clear winner. But play the field too long, and one day you'll wake up forty years old, and all the good ideas will either be married or dating twenty-five-year-olds.

Yes, of course, the grass always looks greener on the other side of the desk—the one with the list of story ideas you're not currently working on. And there's nothing wrong with a little fantasizing. Even Alison Pace, the author of *If Andy Warhol Had a Girlfriend*, who's never had a problem committing to her idea, admits that occasionally her mind drifts to what could have been. "I sometimes daydream about other ideas when I'm having trouble with the current project. I try to see it as an incentive: Finish this book, and you can start the next one." An excellent technique. As with dating, you're not committing for the rest of your life. There's plenty of time for that other great idea—*after* you've finished this book.

Rule #8: Use your friends, but don't abuse your friends.

You know that friend you have, the one who makes you do a play-by-play with her after every date and then every phone conversation, e-mail, and text message that is relevant to said date? Don't be her. When you're dating someone new, it's perfectly natural to sound off with your friends, but don't abuse the privilege. The same goes for your chick lit novel. Working out the kinks in your idea is one thing.

Asking every once in a while if something is funny is fine, too. But if you bounce every plot twist, every laugh line, every dubious turn of phrase off your friends, they will start to screen your calls and block your e-mails.

Rule #9: Rejection happens.

You're out there, you're dating, you're having fun, and then all of a sudden, he puts the kibosh on your courtship. You don't lock yourself in your home (at least not for more than a day or two) and never send yourself out into the world again. Do you? No. Eventually, you try to meet someone else. And one day, because we live in a relatively benevolent universe, you do.

That's how you need to face a rejection—whether it's from an agent, contest judge, or editor. Sometimes the best thing to do is take whatever advice was given in your rejection letter and rework that manuscript; in other cases, you might want to start something brand new and come back to the first story later. Carole Matthews did just that. "I have two rejected manuscripts that I'd love to go back to one day," she told us. "They were submitted to my agent before I was published. He loved them both, but felt they needed something extra. I decided not to rework them at that point, but to move on to a new novel (which turned out to be *Let's Meet on Platform 8*) that incorporated all the elements he felt were missing in those first two. He sold that one within a week of delivery. So, I guess I reacted to the rejection by taking away the positive comments, digesting them, and then working them into my next book." Carole didn't give up, and neither should you. If you give up at the first rejection, then you're selling your book—and yourself—short.

FIVE

No More Excuses, Missy

✳ ✳ ✳

So you want to get a book published. And you're assuming (hoping) that there's a trick to making it happen.

There is. (Drumroll, please.) *Finishing it.*

Many, many people say they want to write a book. But only a small percentage actually finish one. So if you can get to the last page, then you're way ahead of the crowd. But that's the tough part, right? How do you finish it? Do you just turn on your computer and begin writing? Will the words flow from you like beer on tap until you type "The End" with a flourish?

"People often ask me for advice on writing a book," says international bestselling author and chick lit pioneer Marian Keyes. "Because I'm a published author, they assume I'm in on some big secret. But the good news is that there's no big secret . . . and the bad news is that there's no big secret."

Not only is there no easy way to get your book done, but there is only one way: Word by word. Page by page. Chapter by chapter. Writer's block be damned.

Intimidating? Maybe. Luckily for you, we've gathered some tried-and-true methods to make the work less daunting. The plan of action for you will depend on the kind of person you are. Are you easily overwhelmed? A mess? A procrastinator? Trust us, we've heard every excuse. And maybe even said a few ourselves. But no matter what your excuse, if you want to write a book, you can.

49

Words of Wisdom

"I won't say there's no such thing as a natural talent, but after working with many authors over the years, I can offer a few observations: Having natural ability doesn't seem to make writing any easier (and sometimes makes it more difficult), having all the feeling in the world will not ensure the effective communication of feeling on the page, and finally, the degree of one's perseverance is the best predictor of success."—*The Forest for the Trees*, by Betsy Lerner

The Overwhelmed

"It's too much!" you scream. "How am I ever going to write an entire novel? That's like three hundred pages! Do you know how much has to happen in that many pages!?"

OK, calm down. Take a deep, slow breath. Very good. Now remember this: Rome wasn't built in a day, and your book won't be either. You have to break it down into smaller, more manageable tasks. Like this: Today you're going to write five hundred words. If you write only five hundred words (about two pages) every day, in six months you will have a complete draft of your novel.

Lynda Curnyn, author of *Confessions of an Ex-Girlfriend*, vouches for this technique. "The best writing advice I ever got was on a date with a guy who was a writer. And though I hate to give him credit (mostly because he, uh, never called for a second date), he did say that the way he had written his own novel was by simply putting down two pages a day, no matter what. Just fill two pages. So that's what I did. And it worked! You can't wait for inspiration."

If you wake up every morning telling yourself that today you have to write a novel, you'll probably end up pulling that duvet right back over your head. If you wake up telling yourself that today you have to write five hundred words . . . that doesn't seem so hard, does it? The last e-mail you wrote to your best friend was practically five hundred words.

The Instant Gratification Addict

> *"It's going to take me* how *long to finish a book?*
> *Are you crazy?"*

You're the type of girl who stands over the pot waiting for the water to boil. You buy all your books in hardcover. You can't wait for anything. How are you possibly going to work on a project that could take as long as a year? You're not overwhelmed—you're impatient.

Solution (not so different from The Overwhelmed): Set reachable goals. If your goal of the day is to write two pages, once you hit your mark you'll feel a major sense of accomplishment. Lynn Messina, author of *Fashionistas*, agrees: "On days when I'm home writing, I begin at 10 and finish around 6. When I'm starting a new book, I give myself a five-hundred-word minimum for the day, and if things happen to go freakishly well and I hit five hundred words by, say, 11:15, then I get to take the rest of the day off with a clear conscience (hello, TV)."

If your impatience rears its testy little head, you can appease it the way Messina does. "The deeper I get into a book, the higher the daily word count, until I'm three-quarters of the way through and just want to be done already. Then I start earlier in the morning, go later at night, and stop only when I'm too sick of myself to keep going."

It Happened to Me, or Having Fun with Excel

I'm the type of girl who makes a lot of lists, mostly for the pleasure of ticking items off. If you're a real instant gratification addict like me, make a project schedule. This helps keep you in line but also lets you feel that rush of a completed job.

SCHEDULE FOR NEW BOOK

	Mon.	Tues.	Wed.	Thurs.	Fri.	Week Total
Week 1	3,000	3,000	3,000	3,000	3,000	15,000
Week 2	3,000	3,000	3,000	3,000	3,000	15,000
Week 3	3,000	3,000	3,000	3,000	3,000	15,000
Week 4	3,000	3,000	3,000	3,000	3,000	15,000
Week 5	3,000	3,000	3,000	3,000	3,000	15,000
Week 6	3,000	3,000	3,000	3,000	3,000	15,000
					Total	90,000

When I'm writing my first draft, as you can see, I aim to write three thousand words a day, five days a week.* If I have some

---

*FARRIN: *Uh, Sarah, 3K words a day is a lot. And I think writing a book in six weeks will look daunting. Can we massage these numbers a bit?*

other type of event on the day, I'll adjust the daily count to whatever I feel is reasonable.

Now here's where I admit to being a *real* freak. I also make myself a daily schedule that looks a lot like this:

TIME	GOAL
9–10	500
10–11	500
11–12	500
12–1	Lunch
1–2	500
2–3	500
3–4	500
4–5	Read over contracts
5–6	Web site updates
Total	3,000

The truth is, only about twice in my life have I perfectly followed my daily schedule. I discover someone's blog and feel the need to read every entry ever written since its creation. I

SARAH: *But that's what my schedules actually look like.*
FARRIN: *Have you ever actually finished a book in six weeks?*
SARAH: *Um, no, not that I can remember.*
FARRIN: *Perhaps we need a section called Deluded Overachiever?*

decide to order books on Amazon. My mom calls. By the end of the day, my schedule looks more like this:

TIME	GOAL	COMPLETED
9–10	500	520
10–11	500	505
11–12	500	500
12–1	Lunch	Lunch
1–2	500	450
2–3	500	125
3–4	500	0
4–5	Read over contracts	0
5–6	Web site updates	0
Total	3,000	2,100

Which means I'll either have to make up the nine hundred words the next day, or on the weekend, or increase my project schedule by an extra week (which is what normally happens unless I'm under a severe deadline). Either way, having the schedule gives me short-term goals to look forward to, and allows me to procrastinate for the first bit after turning on my computer. Because I can't start writing until I make my chart, right?—*SM*

The Procrastinator

> *"I am going to write a book. I am. Right now. OK,*
> *not right now, but as soon as I'm done cleaning the*
> *egg holders in my refrigerator . . ."*

Most writers consider themselves procrastinators. So how do they get past it?

Here's the thing about writing: It's not a team effort.* No one will pick up your slack. So if you don't do it yourself, it ain't gonna get done.

It's all you, baby. Now get to it.

Of course, it's easier said than done, and we know you might need more than a pep talk from us. So try a Big Mac. Seriously. It worked for Johanna Edwards, author of *The Next Big Thing*. "I'm the world's worst procrastinator. I'm also on a perpetual diet. So whenever I'm in a crunch and I really need to get some writing done, I allow myself to eat some of the junk foods I usually avoid, like pizza or McDonald's. It's not healthy, but it sure does motivate me."

"When I first started writing seriously, right after college, I motivated myself with donuts. I had trouble getting out of bed to write, so I would get up, walk to the donut store, buy two donuts, bring them home, turn on my computer, and start eating and writing. By the time the second donut was consumed, I was into

---

Unless, of course, it is. Some of your favorite chick lit books might have been written by a team. The #1 New York Times *bestseller* The Nanny Diaries? *A team effort by Emma McLaughlin and Nicola Kraus, who believe that working as a duo is a terrific way to keep their writing on track. And we agree. There's nothing like someone waiting for you to finish a chapter to get you to that computer.*

my work. I did that for about a year. And since then, I've been able to do it without the donuts. If I did that now, I'd weigh six hundred pounds."—Sarah Dunn, author of *The Big Love*

Feel free to try this write-and-reward program with shoes. Or television. Or a bath. Anything that gets you to that computer will work.

The Obsessive Perfectionist

"How am I ever going to move on to chapter 2 when I've already spent five months on chapter 1 and it's still not perfect?"

We understand that you want to love your first chapter. That you want it to be the best first chapter ever written. But if you keep tinkering, and rewriting, and second guessing, you will never finish your book.

You need to move on. Don't worry, you can always come back. You're not locking the file—you're just closing it. For now.

Words of Wisdom

"I wish there were an easier, softer way, a shortcut, but this is the nature of most good writing: that you find out things as you go along. Then you go back and rewrite. Remember: No one is reading your first drafts."—*Bird by Bird*, by Anne Lamott

While some writers, like Cara Lockwood and Lynda Curnyn, revise as they write, others, like Caren Lissner (and the prolific half of yours truly), "just let it all pour out." Lissner, who says she's afraid of forgetting essential parts of the plot, powers through her first draft as quickly as possible. "I write and write and write and write. The extra description and shading will often come in later. I sometimes leave Xs and holes to fill in eventually. I just want to get everything out that's in my head."

Your most important goal is to get that first draft out. If you can revise as you write and keep moving forward, that's fantastic. Yay, you. But if you've been fixated on a sentence on page 2 for three months, you might be an obsessive perfectionist, and you desperately need a new strategy. One that favors *writing* over *tinkering*. So here's our advice: Stop obsessing and get back to writing. There will be plenty of time to make each sentence shine.

The Mess

"I've already written two hundred pages," you whine. "But my stuff is all over the place. I wrote twenty pages about Scruffy the dog, but then I realized Scruffy should be a cat!"

Stop. Just stop. You need an outline. *Most* people need outlines. This does not make you an unnatural writer. This makes you a prepared writer. Even the chick lit queen, Sophie Kinsella, author of the massively successful *Shopaholic* series, plots before she begins. "I spend weeks and months plotting and planning and gathering ideas and jokes and thoughts . . . the process usually takes longer than the actual writing itself! So I have a blueprint before I start."

It Happened to Me

Anyone who knows me knows I'm a total mess. Which is why I always outline before I write. When I first get a book idea, I write a half-page outline. Then I write a rough draft of my first three chapters. Once those are done, I create an eight- to sixteen-page outline. I do this because, contractually, I usually have to submit an outline—but also because if I didn't, my novels would end up looking a lot like my desk: an explosion of papers/bills/loose change/napkins and Post-It notes.—*SM*

Since the outline is for your eyes only, don't worry about form, style, following it to a T, and so on. Its purpose is to guide you from one chapter to the next, so as you create it you should focus on the plot and character development. If, while you're writing, you realize you need to stray from it, stray away. Your outline isn't set in stone.

YOUR OUTLINE, YOUR SELF

How you set up your outline—a cohesive paragraph, a numbered list, or a high school–approved roman-numerals-and-letters affair—is up to you, but here is a basic foundation to start with:

* Write out the major events that happen in your story on index cards or Post-Its or on-screen. You can use bullet points, paragraphs, numbered lists, whatever comes naturally to you.

* Your goal is to include major events from the beginning to the end of your story, but you don't have to put each scene in order just yet.

* Give yourself leeway to use shorthand or detailed specifics. You might even throw in bits of dialogue. The amount of detail you provide is up to you.

Now put the events in order, paying attention to pace and plot so you have a preliminary sense of how one scene leads to another. See? Simple. *Now go do it.*

The Commitment-Phobe

> *"I've started five novels. But I can't get past page 3*
> *on any of them! What's wrong with me?"*

Here's the problem. When the going gets tough—you get running.

You have lots of steam at the beginning, but as soon as the love phase is over (i.e., he left the toilet seat up *again*), you want to jump ship to the next idea.

Here's the truth: Every idea, every novel, is going to have rough patches. If you don't learn to plow through them, you will never finish your book.

This rough spot might happen after the second page, or it could happen halfway through the book. Either way, it's much easier to soldier on when you have (here it is again, folks!) *an outline*. Because then you'll know where you're going. Caren Lissner agrees. "Have a good idea of how your novel will end before you begin it. Too many people start out with a lot of steam and then die out because they don't have a really fantastic ending that they're working toward." Knowing your ending will propel you forward. (You can change that ending at any point, as long as you don't stop writing.)

Let's say you have an outline. And you're merrily writing along when you hit smack into a scene that you don't feel like writing. Maybe it's a pivotal moment in the character's development. Or maybe it's a sex scene and frankly, you're just not in the mood. You're inclined to cry writer's block and turn off your computer even though you've only written seventy-eight words today, and to try again tomorrow.

Our first recommendation is to just write it. If it's horrible, you can rewrite it later. At least you'll have something on the page to work with.

But let's say you *really* don't want to write that tough scene today. Instead of not writing at all, dive into a scene that you *are* in the mood for. You can go back to that other scene tomorrow. Or next week. Or once the rest of your book is done. But please, don't dump the whole project because of one rough spot.

> **"I don't believe in writer's block any more than I believe in dieter's block. Either you get your ass in gear and do it, or you putz around. I usually get my ass in gear."**—Alisa Valdes-Rodriguez, author of *The Dirty Girls Social Club*

The Insecure

> *"Everything I write is crap. I am never going to be a published writer. I am no good. Every other chick lit book is better than mine."*

Know this: Every writer is insecure. Even the biggies like Sophie Kinsella. "With every book I write there is a time, midway through, when I hate all the characters, hate the plot, can't believe I came up with such a ridiculous premise, and want to give up! But with any insecurity I think you just have to keep going, keep looking forward, and trust your original instincts."

When Cara Lockwood was writing her first book, *I Do (But I Don't)*, she admits to picking it up occasionally and wondering, "Was I drunk when I wrote this? It's horrible! No one who isn't drunk will want to read this. Maybe I could sell it at a liquor store? No, no, no. I'm just going to throw it away."

But she kept going, finished it, and got it published.

We've said it before, and we'll say it again: Your first draft is not supposed to be perfect. If you go into it thinking that way, you'll never get it done. You need to allow yourself to write a draft that's less than perfect—and maybe even nowhere near it. Because if you've got nothing on the page, you've got nothing to work with. You can't edit a blank page. Your first goal should be to write out that first draft. Your second can be to make it not suck.

> "Don't be surprised if your first efforts are shockingly bad. Indeed, expect to marvel at the gap between what you want to say in your head and how it appears on the page. But persevere; chances are it will improve."—Marian Keyes, author of *Sushi for Beginners*

Lockwood squashed her inner high school girl by enlisting the help of a "writing cheerleader" to keep her going. If you want a cheerleader of your own, pick someone you trust (a well-read friend, relative, or spouse) who will encourage you to finish by telling you what they love about your chapters. Lockwood's friend Shannon ordered her to continue writing. "When I got discouraged, Shannon would tell me that I was funny, talented, and that I might have lost weight."

Make sure your writing cheerleader is someone you trust to be dogged and whom you won't second-guess. And don't get mad at her (or him) for harassing you for the next chapter—that's part of the job.

The Really Busy

> *"I have two kids and a full-time job. I want to write a book, but how am I ever going to find the time to do it? When I have that extra hour in my day, shouldn't I be doing something more productive? Like laundry?"*

If J. K. Rowling can do it, so can you. If you want to write badly enough, you will have to make it a priority. Be a professional: See it as a part-time job, not something you squeeze in between your day job, meeting friends for a drink, and watching TV. Writing is something you should make time for every day, if possible. If you're a morning person, maybe you could designate an hour before work as your writing time. If you're nocturnal, sit down and write every night before bed. If you can put yourself on a schedule and write at the same time every day, it will become part of your routine.

Excuses put away now? Ready to begin? Excellent. But first finish reading our book. Since you paid for it and all. And since we powered through all of *our* excuses and wrote this next section especially for you.

PART TWO

The Details

SIX

What I Like About Me: Creating Your Main Character(s)

✳ ✳ ✳

The single most important element of your chick lit novel is your main character. No matter what kind of story you're aiming to write—whether it's serious or funny, over-the-top or subdued, roman à clef or satire—your protagonist can make or break it.

What readers love about chick lit is that the heroine is *them*—but with more attitude, more courage, or maybe just more shoes. She is Everywoman, with quirks and problems that are believable yet larger than life. She's confident yet insecure. Smart but naïve. Lovable yet flawed. How you create her will depend largely on who you are and whom you've come into contact with in your life. The choices you make for her are as individual as you are. We'd love to be able to offer you a checklist to follow or a list of rules, because we're givers; unfortunately, it's not that simple. You can't just fill in the blanks and end up with the perfect chick lit heroine. But we *can* give you some advice as well as a list of common mistakes—a sort of checklist of things *not* to do.

Like You but Funnier

"When I write a character, I sometimes feel like I'm dropping tiny personality crumbs to mark a trail that starts with me but twists off into the wilderness," says Kristin Gore, whose *Sammy's Hill* took a successful leap from the usual chick lit world of New York publishing to the steps of Capitol Hill. "I want to go somewhere new, but I also want to make sure I can find my way back."

She's not alone. Most authors admit that although they're not always consciously creating their protagonists in their image, sometimes they can't help it. There's a little bit of them in their main characters (or even their secondary characters), and that's just the way it is. Nothing to be ashamed of. But try to remember: You're writing fiction. Of course you're going to draw on what you know and who you are; but don't be afraid to veer off in a direction that's completely unlike you. You and your main character could share some qualities, but she doesn't have to *be* you. The idea for her might spring out of your own anal-retentiveness, for example, but that might be the only thing you two have in common.

Don't be afraid to use yourself or material from your life, but also don't be lulled into thinking that every thought and interaction you've had is comedy gold. In fact, here's an important rule to remember: Just because it happened to you doesn't mean it belongs in your novel. This holds true for things that seem funny or cute or brilliant but just don't translate on the page or serve the story or character. That minor health problem that provides endless fodder for your family might be off-putting in your novel unless you treat it in just the right way. The doddering old tour guide you had at the botanical gardens, the one who talked on and on but didn't make much sense, might have seemed hilarious at the time, but in fiction she could just be . . . boring.

Wonderful though you may be, we can pretty much guarantee that you aren't perfect. Nobody is. Which is why your protagonist shouldn't be either. Who wants to read about a woman with a perfect life? Where's the drama in that? That's why Everywoman will always win out over Ms. Perfect in the battle of appealing heroines. The key is to strike a balance. You don't want your heroine to be so incompetent, for example, that she's frustrating to read about. But she has to be flawed to some extent, because she needs to develop as a character—whether she's developing a spine, her softer side, or any other of a number of qualities; that's part of the fun of reading about her.

> "If you're comfortable writing autobiographical fiction, well, writing in the first person plus honesty basically gives you your main character—you. It helps if you're funny and interesting and willing to humiliate yourself."—Sarah Dunn, author of *The Big Love*

Listen to Your Character

Even though your heroine is your creation, it's possible for her to be wiser than you about certain things, so don't ignore her. It's not like she's going to jump off the page, A-ha video style, and start telling you your business (if this does occur, step away from the computer and maybe get some fresh air—clearly you're working too hard). But if you start putting words into her mouth that really don't belong, she'll let you know.

We can't stress this enough: Don't force your character to behave a certain way simply because that's what you need her to do to make the story move from point A to point Hopeful Ending. If it doesn't feel true, you may need to rework that particular plot point. Surely you've read books (we're not going to name names here) where you've thought, *Why would she say that?* or *Why wouldn't she just go into the restaurant?*

> "If something comes out of a character's mouth that makes you wonder if she'd say that, chances are, she wouldn't say that. You have to go back and 'listen' and revise."—Lynda Curnyn, author of *Confessions of an Ex-Girlfriend*

If you don't pay attention, you run the risk of creating a flawed character (and not in a good way) and leaving readers as confused as this *Publishers Weekly* reviewer felt about a recent chick lit heroine: "Unfortunately, Hannah is inconsistent as a character and a narrator, wavering between savvy and naïveté, between embracing the spotlight and hiding behind the scenes." In addition to trusting your character, another way to avoid this pitfall is to have a solid grasp on who your character is, which, conveniently, we discuss in the very next section.

To Plan or Not to Plan: The Character Sketch

You've probably settled on a general main character for your chick lit story, you know she'll be around a certain age, and you've nailed down one or two of her issues, but is that enough to go on? Is that enough to start writing? Yes and no.

A lot of writers take that vague notion and run with it, filling in the blanks as they write and going back to smooth out the rough spots in the revision process. Melissa Senate's *The Breakup Club* has four main characters, one of whom—a bride who walked into the subway instead of down the aisle just hours before her wedding— Senate struggled with from the very beginning. "From the time I wrote the proposal, I was never sure if I wanted her to go back to her groom or not," Senate says. "I decided to figure it out while writing, but my ambivalence turned the character—and the people in her life—blah. When I delivered the manuscript, my editor told me to rework her. I wanted my editor to just tell me how, but she wouldn't. It had to come from me. When I finally decided what this character wanted from her own life, I was able to write her story and all was well."

To avoid the problem Senate had with her runaway bride (and runaway character), try some advance planning: Complete a character sketch. Both Alisa Valdes-Rodriguez (*The Dirty Girls Social Club*) and Laura Caldwell (*Burning the Map*), writers whose styles are quite different, swear by the character sketch as a way to stay in control. They each start out with a detailed outline and thorough character descriptions. "A lot of my writing is done when I'm not actually putting anything on paper," says Valdes-Rodriguez. "I ride my bike, or drive, and I think. I get a feel for the shape and color of what I'm about to tackle before I do anything. Then I do character sketches, down to the scars they have and what they're from. Every little detail. I guess because I was a newspaper writer, I like to have the people in my novels as real to me as possible, so I write these long back-stories for them. Most of it I don't even end up using, but it helps me to know who they are."

Caldwell works in much the same way: She starts with a concept and a vague idea of a character, and then fills in all the blanks before she jumps into the writing. "For my book *The Year of Living Famously*," she explains, "I knew I wanted to write about this struggling fashion designer who meets a struggling Irish actor, and I knew I wanted the actor to become wildly famous right after they marry. I knew that the designer would hate being a celebrity, and her husband would love it, and the book would be about the tests of a marriage when überfame is tossed into the mix. Once I had that, I had to figure out who these people were."

Caldwell says she won't start writing until she knows all she needs to know about her character, even though this part of the process tends to drag. She asks herself all sorts of questions, from mundane to momentous, and slowly fills in her sketch, answer by answer. Who the character's first love was, who she voted for in the last election, how many glasses of wine she can have before she hits fall-down drunk . . . No detail is too big or too small. "I am usually itching to get into the actual writing of a book. But I know if I patiently complete the sketch and wait to start the story when it's done, the book will be so much better for it, so much more fleshed out and full."

It's this kind of legwork that ensures characters who are fully developed and realistic. What might seem like busywork will pay off in the end.

THE CHARACTER SKETCH

You have to create a character sketch that will work for you, filled with all the information you'd want to know about your character. To get you started, here are some preliminary details for you to figure out. Just fill in the second column, and you'll be on your way to getting to know your main character.

Name	
Age	
Physical description	
Education	
Five words that describe her personality	
Where does she work? Is she good at her job? Why? Or why not?	
Her dream job, or dream life	
Things that annoy her	
Her bad habits	
What people like about her	
Her roadblocks to happiness	

The person she trusts most (and why)	
The person she *should* trust most (and why)	
Her dream guy	
What she does to relax	
Before the book began, the best day of her life	
The worst day of her life	

The Character Arc

As of page 1, you're sending your character on a journey. What do you follow on a journey? A path. (Sure, you could have said "a map," "directions," "street signs," or "the person in front of you," but the answer we're looking for is "a path." Thanks for playing.) In a novel, that path is often referred to as an "arc." Your main character starts in one place and ends up in another, and the novel tells us what happens in between: how she gets from beginning to end (or, in some cases, end of relationship to new beginning)—how she grows as a person.

Part of what guides her on this path is the conflict between what she *wants* and what she *needs*. In a chick lit novel, she usually starts out convinced something is missing from her life, or she finds herself in a situation where something has clearly been taken away—a guy, a job, an apartment, the opportunity of a lifetime. She goes in pursuit of what she wants only to discover it's often the last thing she needs.

In *Milkrun*, for example, Jackie Norris knows what she wants, and it's to get back together with her ex. As the book progresses and

Jackie gets to know herself better, she realizes that what she needs is to be on her own.

Sometimes a character knows exactly what she needs at the beginning, but she loses sight of it along the way, losing sight of herself, and only rediscovers it toward the end of the novel as she's sifting through the wreckage of her life.

Identifying what motivates your protagonist on these two levels will not only help you get to know her but will also help you sketch her character arc, since the tension between want and need will play a crucial part in her eventual epiphany. Don't just answer these questions and forget about them: write the answers down. A Post-It that says simply, "My character wants [blank], but what she really needs is [blank]," will suffice. Put it somewhere visible, so you can always refer to it when you're writing. That way you'll never lose track of where your character is heading.

While all chick lit novels are different, an archetypal chick lit character arc follows the main character's journey from status quo to unhappiness back to satisfaction. If we were plotting *Milkrun* for example, it would look something like this:

HAPPINESS LEVEL

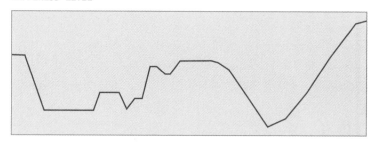

At the beginning of the book, the main character thinks she's happy. And that's when the bomb hits her—in this case her boyfriend breaks up with her via e-mail. Her life slowly starts to improve (with various blips of unhappiness) until toward the end of the novel, when she has her ultimate low. And only after that does the heroine realize what she *needs*, which leads to her finally finding true satisfaction.

Every book and character is going to have a different arc. Highs and lows will vary in length. Drops and climbs will occur in different places. Perhaps the character's "bomb" happens right before the novel begins, or not until halfway through. But when you're writing, you want to make sure your story hits these points:

- The drop: If nothing upsets your character's life, then she has no reason to grow.
- The climb: She could be moving toward a true or a false high, but she's moving on up.
- The blips: Don't make the journey too smooth. Readers want conflict.
- The ultimate low: When everything crashes around the main character, and she hits rock bottom.
- The final climb: She's figuring out how to solve or deal with her problems.
- The satisfied ending: She's happier with her life—or at least on her way to getting there.

Traps: Don't Fall into Them

You know you've encountered one—a main character so off-putting that you don't want to stick with her for even a chapter, let alone an entire novel. In chick lit, some common tropes have been used and abused to the point where they're not only unoriginal—they're unreadable. Herewith, a few of our (least) favorites:

The Improbable Ditz

She is likably naïve but then ends up seeming too accomplished. Of course someone who's a failure in one department might be competent in another (that's the premise of most romantic comedies, after all—"she's the most successful matchmaker in the universe, but when it comes to her own love life, she wouldn't know Mr. Right if she spilled her coffee on him . . ."), but when you're matching these two conflicting qualities, make sure the pieces fit together. Listening to your character's voice will go a long way toward avoiding this trap.

Multiple Personality Mary

This one's another case where listening to your character, and maybe following the character-sketch plan, could really help. MPM's behaviors and actions don't mesh with each other—she is clearly self-absorbed, and the only magazine she reads is *Us Weekly*, yet she makes sure to spend every third Sunday volunteering at her local Young Democrats chapter and is about to plan a peace really—resulting in quizzical looks from your readers, which isn't how you want your readers looking. (Rapt. That's what you're going for. Rapt. And smiling.)

The Bitch

This character has an edge that's a bit too sharp. Of course your character can have attitude, but make her too cold, too calculating, too bitter, too bitchy, and you risk turning off your readers. If the story revolves around the thawing of an ice queen, make sure she doesn't completely alienate readers from the get-go. One self-deprecating line of dialogue or narration or a lesson learned early on can go a long way toward keeping you (and her) on track.

The Doormat

This very sweet girl lets everyone walk all over her and then spends the book whining about it (see also Wendy the Whiner, below). Would you want to read that? What you want is a character who might have been taken advantage of, but it's not terminal—she doesn't let it happen over and over and over throughout the book without any inkling of self-awareness. If your character starts out as a doormat on page 1, you'd better make sure that her arc follows her journey from Doormat to Woman in Control.

Wendy the Whiner

This character complains about everything and has a "the world is out to get me" attitude that hardly seems warranted. She tends to come off as more pathetic than put-upon. Make sure your character's complaints are justified by making her situation more awful than she is.

It Happened to Me

When I turned in my first draft of *Bras & Broomsticks*, one of my editor's comments was that the main character, Rachel, wasn't as likable as she should be. I reread it and realized Rachel did in fact sound harsher than I had intended. My editor kindly pointed out that there's a difference between a character who whines and complains about everything and one who observes the world around her and reports what she finds crazy/stupid/negative in a funny way. So I went back over the manuscript and revised the sections where the main character came across as a brat. Sometimes all it takes is deleting a few sentences here and there.—*SM*

Quirky Beyond Belief

Chick lit is overflowing with quirky characters. Women who are so endearingly odd you'd follow them anywhere. But when the unique behaviors get piled on too high or feel too forced, the character ends up being someone you're more likely to politely ask to stop following you. It's OK to give your character an eclectic hobby, but make sure it suits her and it's believable. And know when to say when. If you make her an amateur ham-radio operator who collects nineteenth-century doilies, Jack La Lanne memorabilia, and bobble-head dolls, you no longer have a character—you have an oddity. Remember the sitcom *Committed*, which was overflowing with quirky characters, including a woman with an old clown living in her closet? No? That's because it was *canceled*.

Perky Patty

Oh, Perky Patty. She suffers from a gee-whiz attitude that feels as if the writer is reaching for naïve and completely missing the mark. PP is channeling Doris Day, not the contemporary Everywoman you want your main character to be. Keep an eye on the perk-o-meter: Sustained high levels can cause serious eye-rolling in your readers.

I Rant, Therefore I Am

It's admirable to have a cause you want to address or an issue you want to demonstrate, or a desire to write subtle social commentary, but characters whose only purpose is to provide a mouthpiece for the author's rant don't make for good fiction. They rarely have the likable, realistic qualities a chick lit heroine needs to succeed. We're not telling you not to include any causes or commentary—we just want you to make sure that you don't lose sight of your story and your character. If your character is fully formed, then she can probably get away with ranting all she wants.

The Incredible Not-Growing Woman

The woman who learns nothing and doesn't change at all throughout the story is not the woman you want at the center of your chick lit novel. Your main character needs to develop. If she ends up in the exact same place she began, then the story hasn't really gone anywhere. And it's spent about three hundred pages and several hours of your readers' time not doing so.

PERKY PATTY   WENDY THE   QUIRKY BEYOND
WHINER   BELIEF

Feeling good about your main character? Ready to meet and make the rest of the people in her life?

SEVEN

Your Friends and Neighbors: Secondary Characters

✳ ✳ ✳

Since your novel isn't a one-woman show, you're going to need secondary characters. Parents, siblings, friends, colleagues, boyfriends, ex-boyfriends, one-night stands, husbands . . . It's a party, and everyone's invited; but the trick to a successful cast of characters is to be selective. You don't need to include everyone your protagonist has ever come in contact with. Better to have a handful and develop them fully: Just because they're secondary, doesn't mean they can be two-dimensional. So how do you get them to stand on their own two feet?

You Again? Clichéd Characters

If you want your secondary characters to feel real, you can't fall back on stereotypes. The bitchy boss? The jerk ex-boyfriend? The gay best friend? The knockout friend whom guys fall head over heels for, leaving your poor protagonist out in the cold? These archetypes might have worked five years ago, but when something has been done again and again, it becomes a cliché.

We're not saying your protagonist absolutely can't have a gay best friend, but he has to be different from all the gay best friends that have existed before him. Maybe he comes out during the novel. Maybe the gay best friend is a woman. Or take the knockout. Maybe she's undergone six different plastic surgeries to get that way. Or maybe she's not good-looking—but guys flock to her anyway. Maybe the boss isn't bitchy but needy and syrupy sweet. Readers enjoy—and relate to—characters that catch them off guard, so go ahead and surprise them.

Make Your Secondary Characters Three-Dimensional

Remember those character sketches we told you about in the previous chapter? They work for secondary characters, too. One way to make your characters break out of the mold is to understand who they are before you start writing. You can do an abbreviated and slightly tweaked character sketch to help get to know them. Use ours as a springboard:

Name	
Age	
Physical description	
Job	
Relationship to the main character? How long have they known each other? How did they meet?	
Five words to describe her/his personality	
Things that annoy her/him	
Her/his bad habits	
Her/his dreams	
Her/his roadblocks to happiness	

If you want readers to care about your characters, they can't come across as cardboard cutouts. Caren Lissner noticed this happening in her novel *Starting from Square Two* and fixed it in a rewrite. "The love interest in my second novel, Todd, is a train conductor," Lissner says. "Right away, I liked that about him because I think freight trains are pretty cool. And I had him say he thinks freight trains are cool, too. But he didn't explain it. People were telling me that they didn't really know much about Todd. So I had Todd give my main character, Gert, a whole explanation of how he ended up in his job and what he likes about it. All that stuff was in my head but not on the page."

If you make your character too one-sided or don't explain why your character is the way she or he is, readers won't buy it. This is especially true for the villains of your book. No one is evil just because. If you want to have a character who's out to get your heroine, fine, but show the reader why. "It's when a character behaves badly in a vacuum that the bounds of believability are stretched," *New York Times* bestselling authors Emma McLaughlin and Nicola Kraus explain. Show why your villain lashes out at your heroine. Even though the villain isn't the book's main event, you need to spend the time and energy to make her or him believable.

> "We find it helps to pose the question, *What stimuli in our character's environment are causing him or her to mistreat our protagonist?* In our first novel [*The Nanny Diaries*], we strove to show that the character Mrs. X, who could be considered villainous by some, would strike out at Nanny only as a direct result of the frustration she felt being neglected by her husband. In our second novel [*Citizen Girl*], we took the same pains with Guy, whose rude treatment of Girl was motivated by his professional pressures."—Emma McLaughlin and Nicola Kraus

Less Is More

We're glad that you made those character sketches. Really. But just because you have doesn't mean you have to include every single little detail in your manuscript. These are secondary characters, after all. We want you to be as familiar with them as possible, but the reader only needs to know enough to make the character feel believable and relevant. You don't need to write pages and pages of backstory for each secondary character; you just need to choose the characters' details and dialogue carefully, and you'll show your reader everything she needs to know.

SARAH IN A NUTSHELL

The best trick I learned in a creative writing class was what I call "The Nutshell Moment." A high school teacher told us to think of one event or action in our lives that defined us. Just one. A studious guy in our class said that when he was a kid he memorized the first fourteen digits of pi. Digits he could still recite ten years later. I told the story of how when I read my first book, *Ramona and Her Father*, I was expecting doodles of balloons on page 100. As in, Congrats! You made it to a hundred! Wahoo! If that anecdote was in a novel, you'd start to get an idea about the character—likes to read, cheerful, possibly craves approval or rewards . . .

※ Think about what your personal moment is.

※ Ask your friends and family what their "moment" is (a worthy personality test for potential boyfriends perhaps?).

※ Now try to come up with nutshell moments like these for each of your characters.

Raison d'Être

Your book should not be a random compilation of everything you've ever thought and every person you've ever known. Each character has to be there for a reason, and the reason shouldn't be because she screwed you in real life and now you're getting even.

Maybe she's the antagonist. The antagonist faces off against your protagonist. In a chick lit mystery like Lynda Curnyn's *Killer Summer* or Jennifer Weiner's *Goodnight Nobody*, we're talking about the bad guy who tries to take out the heroine. In standard chick lit, think about the characters who are pitted against the protagonist, like Mrs. X in *The Nanny Diaries*, Miranda in *The Devil Wears Prada*, Darcy in *Something Borrowed*.

The conflict between the protagonist and the antagonist is what often drives the plot of the novel forward, leading to the story's climax. (No worries, there's more on plot and conflict in chapter 9.) Antagonists—or in their more evil incarnations, villains—are always more interesting when they're multidimensional. Emily Giffin spent a lot of time fine-tuning Darcy in *Something Borrowed*. "She was self-centered, superficial, and self-indulgent, but I never viewed her as evil or one-dimensional. I wanted to be sure that she was not a flat character devoid of depth or warmth. In my revisions, I worked at softening some of her edges." And who knows? If your antagonist becomes especially fascinating, maybe she'll deserve her own sequel, as Darcy got in *Something Blue*. One day it occurred to Giffin that she ought to tell Darcy's version of events. "After all," Giffin says, "There are two sides to every story."

Secondary characters that act as foils are also pitted against the protagonist, but more subtly. These characters are usually her friends or colleagues. Melissa Senate uses this type of character to highlight her protagonist's personality. In her first book, *See Jane Date*, the foil, Natasha, is the main character's high school nemesis, a glam actress whose memoirs Jane is stuck editing and who makes Jane feel like crapola for living in a dumpy tenement studio, wearing dowdy work clothes, and having the word *assistant* in her title. But Jane and the foil slowly become friends as Jane realizes Natasha isn't as perfect as she appears. In *Whose Wedding Is It Anyway?*, the spin-off to *See Jane Date*, the foil is the main character Eloise's coworker. Both are newly engaged and getting free weddings sponsored by the magazine they work for, but Eloise isn't sure she wants to get married, while the foil is a gushing, blushing bride who makes Eloise feel even worse about her ambivalence.

Everything Is Related

Even if you've come up with some fabulous foils and terrifying villains, you can't just throw them into the story and expect them to exist side by side. They have to relate to each other in a believable way.

Say your story involves three BFFs (best friends forever, 'natch); it should be clear why these people are friends. Regardless of how you create this—shared history, shared interests, shared living space—readers shouldn't feel as if they've just stumbled into that episode of *The Twilight Zone* where five strangers all appear in the same room and have no clue who they are, why they're there, or how the hell to escape.

When you're writing, consider how you connect with people—what brings you together and what pulls you apart. Think about:

- How you met your best friend or your boyfriend.
- What you fight with your sister about.
- Why, out of all the people in your office you're friendly with, there are only two you actually see outside of work.
- How some people *get* you and others never will.

These are but a few subjects to consider. If you take the time to ask yourself questions and work on this material, either before you get started or as you're writing, you'll find that you *get* your characters.

FAMILY TREE

Create a chart of the main character and secondary characters in your story.

* Put your main character in the middle of the page, surrounded by the names of your secondary characters.

* Make sure that each secondary character has a line connecting to the main character and that you can explain that line (e.g., sister-in-law) and qualify it (e.g., married to main character's brother for three years; highly critical of main character's lifestyle).

* Now draw lines between the secondary characters and explain how they know each other and what they think of each other.

* Your diagram could look like the one on page 86, based on four characters from Sarah's novel *Me vs. Me*.

Different Strokes for Different Folks

You know how sometimes when you're watching a new TV show you can't tell the actors apart because they all have brown hair, medium builds, and big smiles? The same thing happens to readers when characters are not clearly defined. Not necessarily with physical descriptions, but with who they are. Fictional characters, like real people, won't act, react, and sound the same. The most valuable writing lesson Lynn Messina has learned is that "different characters have to respond to the same stimuli in their own unique and entirely personal way."

She applied that lesson in her novel *Mim Warner's Lost Her Cool*, when three characters, Mim, Ian, and Meghan, find themselves hiding from a murderer. When the murderer leaves and they all

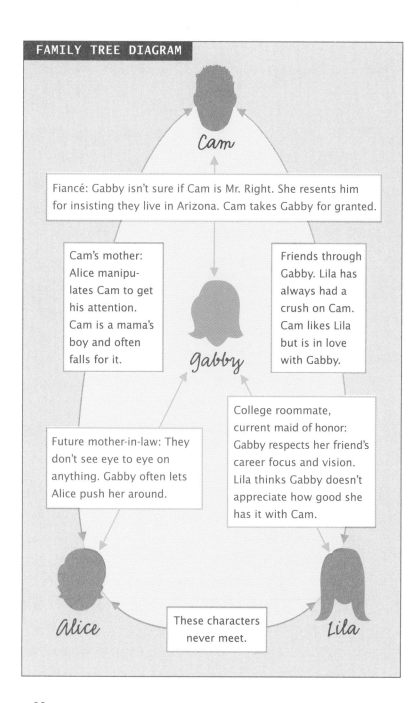

FAMILY TREE DIAGRAM

Cam

Fiancé: Gabby isn't sure if Cam is Mr. Right. She resents him for insisting they live in Arizona. Cam takes Gabby for granted.

Cam's mother: Alice manipulates Cam to get his attention. Cam is a mama's boy and often falls for it.

Friends through Gabby. Lila has always had a crush on Cam. Cam likes Lila but is in love with Gabby.

Gabby

Future mother-in-law: They don't see eye to eye on anything. Gabby often lets Alice push her around.

College roommate, current maid of honor: Gabby respects her friend's career focus and vision. Lila thinks Gabby doesn't appreciate how good she has it with Cam.

Alice

These characters never meet.

Lila

abandon their hiding spots, each character reacts in a different way that illustrates something about her or his personality. Mim, who is the reason they're all there, tries to complete her mission. Ian focuses on how they can get out without leaving false clues for the police (because nobody wants to go to the cops). Meghan freaks out—other than shaking and trying to catch her breath, she doesn't do anything. "Their responses had to gel with who their characters were," Messina says. "Mim: active but insane. Ian: active but ethical. Meghan: passive."

I SAY *TOMATO*, YOU SAY *TOMAHTO*

Use the following scenario to experiment with creating characters who don't sound exactly alike.

※ Emma has decided that law school isn't for her.

※ She drops out to become a pastry chef, then drops the bomb about her career change at Thanksgiving dinner.

※ She's surrounded by her immediate family, all of whom will react differently.

> ❋ Let's give her a younger brother, older sister, eccentric aunt, sin-
> gle mom, and her mom's brand-new boyfriend.
>
> Write a list showing how each person will take the news and why,
> and make sure each person's reaction is distinct. You can show this in
> dialogue, action, or both. Who will spit their drink out, and who will
> simply say, "Pass the peas"? These are just suggestions, of course;
> you're on your own now.

You should also pay attention to how differently men and women might react or speak. Give the men in your story depth by making them feel like real guys. Easier said than done, sure. But just try to avoid making every guy in the story (save for the gay best friend) a jerk, or the main guy unrelentingly patient, kind, loving, and understanding no matter what is heaped on him. Rework dialogue that feels less like a real man and woman talking and more like a woman and her image of a man talking. Ask your brother, cousin, boyfriend, whoever to read your manuscript with a testosterone-sensitive eye and to mark areas that don't feel true.

The Guy

Speaking of testosterone, you already know that your protagonist doesn't need a ring at the end of the book, but if she does end up with a guy (or the possibility of a guy), there are a few things to consider about how to make him a good catch.

First off, you want your reader to fall in love with him at the same time your heroine does. While working on *Something Borrowed*, Emily Giffin and her editor felt that the love interest wasn't resonating the way they wanted. "Dex was coming across as too smooth, almost slick. This wasn't my intent—I always viewed Dex as a good guy rather than a womanizer. His feelings for Rachel were sincere from the start. So I had to rewrite certain scenes to be sure that was clear to the reader. After all, Rachel's dilemma would have become trivial if her relationship with Dex was merely about sex, intrigue, or getting even with a bad friend." If your reader doesn't like the guy, she isn't going to understand why your protagonist does, simple as that.

This works in reverse as well. If your girl is going to kick her guy to the curb, you want your reader to think she made the right decision. Unless you're trying to create a character who consistently makes the wrong decision. If your character is choosing between two men, you have to make the one she ends up with likable enough throughout so that your reader is rooting for him. Of course, you can't make it too obvious. (And you thought real dating was tricky.)

Your guy doesn't have to be picture-perfect. In fact, he shouldn't be. "Perfect men just aren't believable," says Johanna Edwards. "I always try to give my romantic lead forgivable flaws—things that make him human, yet aren't deal breakers."

Maybe he's misguided, like Brady in Edwards's *Your Big Break*, who is passionately involved in an amateur poetry group where he writes and performs dramatic readings of terrible poems. Maybe he cheats on his fiancée, like Dex in Giffin's *Something Borrowed*. Maybe he's pompous, like Luke in Sophie Kinsella's *Shopaholic* series. Or maybe he just does stupid things, like Stephen in Laura Wolf's *Diary of a Mad Bride*, who after being engaged for four months decides that the wedding date has to be changed from June 2 to June 22 so it won't conflict with the NBA playoffs. The best love interests are the ones we see warts and all (literal warts may be pushing the chick lit boundaries, but hey, if it works for the story . . .). Of course, it's a thin line. Look at *Sex and the City*—we were able to excuse Big's commitment-phobia, but as soon as the Russian hit Carrie, we all knew that was code for "now he has to get the boot."

Where'd You Get That Idea? Using Your Friends

In the same way your main character is you but funnier, your secondary characters are often your friends and family, only funnier. And sometimes blonder, bitchier, dumber, and so on. You may now be wondering how you can keep the real-life role models from freaking out. Just be sure that your characters aren't carbon copies of their real-life counterparts. Shoplift a few items; don't steal the whole store.

The thing about creating characters is that they're often a mishmash of a bunch of different people you know. Robyn Harding admits that some of her characters in *The Journal of Mortifying Moments* are composites of friends, acquaintances, coworkers, and television/movie characters. She got a kick out of everyone's reactions—friends who insisted that the Dave character is so-and-so and Sonja is so-and-so. "The funny thing," says Harding, "was that friends were adamant that they knew who the characters were, but they were all pinpointing different people."

But what if you have a friend who's so ridiculous that you just have to write about her? You may want to consider Stacey Ballis's policy: "If a character is going to be terribly unflattering, better to keep your friends out of it." However, she doesn't think you should worry too much. "Our perception of another human being is almost never specifically accurate, because it's filtered through our own idea of who they are. By the time you write them down, give them voice, they're altered. They've become a tool of your writing." So if you simply have to write about someone, just make sure that you've masked her enough so that she's at least unrecognizable to herself. Just take the crazy and lose the rest.

The Name Game

If all your characters' names are Apple, Brooklyn, and Rumer, your book will sound like the Children of Superstars edition of *Us Weekly*. You can definitely have a unique and interesting name, like Lynn Messina's Vig Morgan in *Fashionistas*, but one such name goes a long way. On the flipside, you don't want all the characters' names sounding alike—if the love interest is named Mike, the gay best friend is Mark, and the brother is Mick, your reader might get confused and think the heroine's sex life is getting a bit . . . creepy.

Don't worry. A character's name is easy to change late in the game (ah, the beauty of find and replace); it's the rest of him you really have to focus on as you write.

EIGHT

Elements of Style
(and We're Not Talking About Fashion)

✳ ✳ ✳

Like choosing the right shoes to go with that cute new skirt, you've got to match your style to your story. That doesn't mean a sad story needs to be told in a sad way; after all, wearing a black skirt doesn't mean you have to wear black shoes. You simply need to consider whether you want your book to be laugh-out-loud funny, steamy, suspenseful, literary . . . or maybe some combination of all of these. You have to choose whether you want it to feel like a long monologue, a chorus of voices, or a lyrical tale. Whatever you decide, you should aim to create your own style, which you can do through tone, point of view, tense, language, dialogue, and description. And while these are all separate elements, each choice you make will likely affect the others.

Tone

Sure, you're writing chick lit. To a good portion of the reading world, this means you must be writing something light and fluffy, the literary equivalent of a marshmallow. But if you've read widely among the vast array of chick lit novels (and we're guessing—and hoping—you have), you know there's much more to it than that. Not that there's anything wrong with light and fluffy—some of our favorites are of that variety. But there are many other ways to tell your story, so make sure to keep your options open. Because your tone will help you create a style that's all yours.

Take *The Big Love*, by Sarah Dunn. At the outset, this is a classic story of girl gets dumped by boy, girl must soldier on. But Dunn's crisp, matter-of-fact voice, which is filled with wit and wisdom in equal parts, distinguishes this tale from the pack of like-minded stories. And yet just because it feels conversational doesn't mean it came easily. "Creating the voice was the trickiest part," admits Dunn, "and it took about a year to get it down." She says she was always conscious of creating a natural voice for her protagonist, Alison, which affected other aspects of her storytelling method. "I wanted it to be the voice of a woman telling a friend of story, and that led me to make a bunch of specific stylistic decisions. For example, there is almost no physical description in *The Big Love*, which drives some people crazy. My theory was that if you tell a friend a story about what happened the night before at a restaurant, you don't describe the wallpaper and the tile floor and the writing on the mirror behind the bar before you get rolling."

Which isn't to suggest that there's absolutely no description whatsoever in *The Big Love*. There is; it just happens to flow so well with her voice that it doesn't hit you over the head with its descriptiveness:

> **There were several things about Andre's appearance on my doorstep that made me feel better, but the most obvious was that he was so clearly in worse shape than I was. I'm not talking about what he was wearing (a green tracksuit), or the fact that he obviously hadn't shaved in some time—rather, that Andre's going to the trouble of tracking me down and knocking on my front door was so plainly an act of complete and utter desperation that I felt relatively sane in comparison.**

With the physical description she does give, Dunn could have told us he had sandy brown hair or that he was tall, but those details don't really matter here. She simply wants the reader to know that Andre looked like a broken man.

In *Summer in the Land of Skin*, Jody Gehrman's main character is wrestling with some serious issues, and while Gehrman's voice is moody and serious, she punctuates her story with flashes of lightness, ably avoiding anything maudlin. She says her setting helped her create just the right feel for her story. "I think of *Summer in the Land of Skin* as a love letter to Bellingham, Washington," she explains. "The landscape itself is moody, and so were my years there, so I wanted to capture that atmosphere." But like most novelists, Gehrman admits she's just as susceptible to overwriting or "veering off into maudlin-ville" as the next girl. To avoid that common pitfall, she enlisted the help of a good friend who also happens to be a good editor. "Tania helped me rein in anything that was over-the-top sentimental or melodramatic. She taught me a lot about restraint."

Lee Nichols was going for something completely different in *Tales of a Drama Queen*—she was aiming for (and achieved) a read that would be downright glee inducing. One method that worked for her was to not let the tone overtake the story. Sure, her aim was to make people laugh, but she knew she wanted—and needed—more than that to make the novel work as, well, a novel. "I try not to indulge in scenes that are only there to make people laugh," she says, adding something you should always keep in mind: that "every scene should be integral to the plot or the main character's growth or story goal." Basically, make every word count.

No matter what your tone, make sure to keep it consistent. You don't want your book to seem like it was written by committee. You can catch most of the inconsistencies during revision time (see chapter 12) with a big, fat, yellow highlighter.

POV

It's not unheard of to start writing a story in the third person only to realize fifty pages in that maybe telling the tale in the first person—directly from the mouth and mind of your protagonist—would have been a better way to go. The opposite can also happen: As John Irving told *Entertainment Weekly*, he wrote the initial version of his novel *Until I Find You* in the first person. It wasn't until a few days after he turned all 820 pages of it in to his editor that he realized what the book needed was some emotional distance, so he spent the next nine months converting it to the third person. Don't ignore these doubts—you're having them for a reason. You have a number of options regarding how to tell your story, and if you're getting the feeling that the one you've chosen isn't the best one, you owe it to yourself to explore other points of view. (See the table on pages 98 and 99.)

The majority of chick lit novels are written in the first person, and many of the writers we spoke to offered similar reasons for this: "Writing in the first person can feel really intimate, and really immediate, and it gives you a way to pull the reader in close," says Sarah Dunn. Jennifer O'Connell, author of *Bachelorette #1*, agrees. "I can't imagine writing in the third person. I know it's cliché, but when writing in the first person it's like channeling the character."

It Happened to Me

Multiple first-person narrators can give your story the jolt it needs. I used this POV in my fourth book, *Monkey Business*. I considered writing it in the third person, but ultimately chose first person to illustrate how each character is stuck in her or his own subjectivity. Once I made that decision, I had to choose who got to narrate. In my first draft, I had a character's girlfriend chime in with her version of the events, but we chopped it in the final draft. My editor felt that having too many perspectives was overkill and confusing, especially since this character was peripheral.—*SM*

When you're writing in the first person, be extra careful about how you present information. Try to avoid obvious exposition, such as "In the mirror I could see my long brown hair, brown eyes, tall frame, orange sweater, and used jeans." The information might be necessary for the reader to know, but you don't want to hit her over the head with it. Try to reveal the description in dialogue or observations that flow naturally in the narration, as in the example from *The Big Love*.

There are plenty of popular chick lit titles told in the third person as well, such as *Smart vs. Pretty* by Valerie Frankel or *Starting from Square Two* by Caren Lissner, so don't worry if the first person doesn't feel right to you.

Less common is a novel told in the second person, the "you" voice. One of the most successful examples is Jay McInerney's *Bright Lights, Big City*. Second person worked for that book, and it could be fun to experiment with, but it might not be the best way to go for your first novel.

Tense

Before chick lit, writing a novel in the present tense was somewhat esoteric, but now it's standard operating procedure. An argument can be made for both past and present, so the choice is really up to you. The present is fresh, immediate, and energetic—all words that have been used to describe chick lit itself. But the past tense allows for more natural reflection. Look at these two examples from popular books to see that both can be effective:

> OK. Don't panic. Don't panic. It's only a Visa bill. It's a piece of paper, a few numbers. I mean just how scary can a few numbers be?—*Confessions of a Shopaholic*, by Sophie Kinsella

POINT OF VIEW	CENTRAL PRONOUN
First Person	**I**: The narrator is the main character
Multiple First Person	**I**: Rotating first person perspectives from a few of the main characters
Third Person Limited	**He, she**: The narrator is in the head of specific characters
Third Person Omniscient	**She, he**: The narrator knows everything everyone is thinking

ADVANTAGES	DISADVANTAGES
☀ Intimate ☀ Confessional tone ☀ Readers likely to empathize, since they are only hearing one side of the story	☀ Limiting ☀ Exposition can seem clunky
☀ Intimate ☀ Confessional tone ☀ You can move from person to person ☀ Since readers can see what multiple people are doing, they'll know more than individual characters do	☀ Readers might confuse characters ☀ Readers will have less time to empathize when there are too many characters
☀ You can move from person to person ☀ Since readers can see what multiple people are doing, they'll know more than individual characters do	☀ Readers might confuse characters if you show more than one viewpoint ☀ Often less intimate than first person
☀ You can move from person to person ☀ Readers can know more than the characters	☀ Readers might confuse characters ☀ Readers will have less time to empathize when there are too many characters

> You know how in scary books a character will say, "I felt my heart stop"? Well, I did. Really. Then I felt it start to pound again, in my wrists, my throat, my fingertips. The hair at the back of my neck stood up. My hands felt icy. I could hear the blood roaring in my ears, as I read the first line of the article: "I'll never forget the day I found out my girlfriend weighed more than I did."—*Good in Bed*, by Jennifer Weiner

Make sure that whatever you decide, you stick with it consistently. It's beyond frustrating to read a manuscript that jumps back and forth between past and present in a completely haphazard way (as opposed to a deliberate switch for narrative purposes, which is A-OK).

Language

It's not news to you that your language informs your writing style, so choose your words carefully and keep the following hints in mind.

Vary word choice.

Remember when your high school best friend would learn a new word and then use it every five minutes? All of a sudden things weren't *extra*—they were *superfluous*. Remember how annoying that was? Don't replicate that behavior in your writing (unless you're making a point of establishing something about the way your character speaks).

Overuse can happen with words both distinctive and plain, and it isn't something you should worry too much about in your first draft. But when you're doing a read-through, circle words that are used often or in close proximity to each other, and when you hit the revision stage, tinker with your sentences to avoid repetition.

Mistakes I've Known

I once read a submission that was interesting, was well-written for the most part, and had an exceedingly likable narrator—except for one thing: her excessive use of the word *exceedingly*. It felt like it was on every page. I'm sure it wasn't, but it appeared enough times to make me think that, which isn't a good sign. It was like a tic, like the author couldn't help but use *exceedingly* to describe, well, everything. I didn't end up buying that manuscript for other reasons, but if I had, going through it and circling all those *exceedingly*s would have been a large part of the editing process.—*FJ*

Don't overwrite.

Purple is a perfectly fine color. Purple prose, however, is not perfectly fine. Your chick lit novel is no place to be flowery, so don't hurt yourself trying to create "fancy" sentences, because chances are an editor will see your attempt as overwrought and icky. You wouldn't want to read this, would you?

> Jane stared longingly at the elegant shoes perched delicately on the mirrored wall. The shimmering crimson heel was stacked like hardcover books waiting to be shelved, and she knew with every desperate fiber of her being that she had to have them ...

Of course, you don't want to underwrite. A novel filled with "See Jane try on shoes. See Jane buy shoes" won't win you any fans, either.

Beware redundancy.

Maybe it's a matter of not knowing what certain words mean; maybe it's a by-product of trying to be as descriptive as possible. Whatever the cause, when you're revising, be sure to rub out redundancies. There's just no reason a sentence should, for example, look like this: "I looked over at her *aquiline, beaklike* nose." Or like this: "She *quietly whispered* in his ear." Whispering implies quietness, so the adverb isn't necessary. Keep your sentences tight and your writing clean by remembering that every word counts.

Verbs are your friends; good verbs are your really good friends.

The verbs you choose have the potential to make your sentences sink or swim. You should choose active, vivid ones and try to refrain from relying only on forms of *to be*. Sure, the girl could *walk away from* the wall she was leaning against, but if she's feeling low and defeated, she might have to *peel herself off* the wall. Or, your narrator could *stand up* when her name is called, but maybe, just maybe, she's particularly eager and *leaps out of her chair*? See what we're getting at? Verbs add color and life to your sentences—as well as to your characters and descriptions—if you let them.

Dialogue

The best way to ensure that your dialogue feels true is to read it out loud. "I hear the characters talking in my head," says Lee Nichols, whose second novel, *Hand-Me-Down*, is high on dialogue that is smart, snappy, and realistic. "Often I find myself saying things aloud as I write. But it's a balancing act to write dialogue that reads like people talk but isn't as mundane as actual conversation can be."

We can't stress enough how crucial it is to work on making your dialogue feel real. Good dialogue can make or break a chick lit book, so you don't want your characters speaking in clichés or having conversations that feel oddly formal, archaic, or unnaturally peppy.

On a nitpicky note, be sure to keep track of how many times your characters call each other by name in one conversation and then consider how many times you actually say someone's name to them when you're chatting.

You should also watch your dialogue tags, those phrases before or after the dialogue that identify who is speaking. It's nice to vary *said* or *says* with some other verbs occasionally, but try too hard and you run the risk of forcing it. You want your reader to get the tone of the conversation, but there are other ways to achieve that. You can, for example, surround your dialogue with action or description. So instead of,

"No," she whimpered. "I won't go."
"Have it your way," he spat.

you could write

"No." She could feel the tears welling in her

eyes. "I won't go."

"Have it your way," he said, dropping her hand and stalking away.

In many cases, you can even forgo the tag when the speaker's identity is clear from the context.

Mistakes I've Known

In one otherwise well-written book I edited, the author was obviously trying to avoid too many instances of *I said*, but what she ended up with was too many occurrences of *I informed him [or her]*. I went through and changed many of them to *said*, and in some cases just deleted the dialogue tag entirely, since it was perfectly clear who was speaking.—*FJ*

Just as we want you to vary your word choices, we also want you to make sure your dialogue doesn't all sound the same. By which we mean: Not all of your characters should speak alike. There's just no way, for example, that your main character, her gay best friend, her mother, and her coffee boy all use the word *terrific* on a regular basis. If you want to make a point (e.g., how disturbing it is that the mother has started saying, "That's hot"), that's one thing. But keep it natural by making sure each character is distinct and realistic.

CHICK LIT MAD LIBS: BAD DIALOGUE

"So, what are you going to do about _____ , _____
[bad situation] [unique woman's
_____?" my best friend asks
name or really cute nickname for a more common name]
me as she fingers her _____ ____ hair.
[adjective] [color]

"Ugh, I do not know, _____ . Do you
[woman's name #2, can also be unusual]
realize what _____ means? It means I'm going to have to
[bad situation]
_____!"
[repercussions of bad situation]

"But you swore you'd never let that happen, _____."
[first woman's name]

"I know, _____," I sniff, "but now that _____
[second woman's name]   [overexplana-
_____ , I have no other choice." I sigh dejectedly and play
tion of bad situation]
with my dessert fork.

"I know something that will cheer you up, _____,"
[first woman's name]
_____ smirks. She has that cat-who-ate-the-canary look
[second woman's name]
on her face.

"What?" I ask curiously.

"Look to your left and check out the _____
[man's body part, preferably buns
_____ on that _____.
or pecs]   [hottie/stud]

I do as _____ says and lock eyes with the most
[second woman's name]
_____ male specimen I've ever seen in real life. "Wow, _____
[adjective]   [second
_____, he's a total _____," I drool. I'd like to be the cat who
woman's name]   [hottie/stud]
gets to eat *that* canary!

Description

What you choose to describe is often as important as how you
describe it. As Jody Gehrman, who has written all of her novels in

the first person, explains, "The lens the protagonist provides is all-important. What she notices in the landscape around her, what she finds funny or sad, who she thinks is hot—these are all details that come together and build the book, moment to moment."

That said, if you're writing in the conversational first person, keep it real by not spending paragraph upon paragraph describing, say, the fabric on the waiting-room couch (unless maybe your protagonist is an interior designer) or the smell wafting in from the kitchen. In the same vein, avoid making your novel into a chick lit procedural, where you describe every move people make, every breath they take, in minute, excruciating detail. When a character leaves the room, we don't always need the play-by-play. This:

> I stood up and crossed the studio. As I approached the door, I reached out to grab the handle. I twisted it and pulled it open, then stepped out into the bright sunlight.

could so easily look like this:

> I left the studio and stepped out into the bright sunlight.

See? Short, sweet, and just as effective. And you won't be boring your reader to tears.

Devices such as similes and metaphors can be wonderful, evocative ways to describe a moment, a feeling, a color, but take care when you use these devices. First of all, you need to make sure the image works. It may sound pretty, but if it doesn't make sense, you're merely wasting words. Your similes or metaphors should help the reader understand what you're describing—not confuse them further. Don't rely on one device too often, either. There's something mildly annoying and frustrating about reading different versions of the same literary device over and over in a novel. It feels as if the writer is being lazy or doesn't have the skill to use other descriptive tools. Sometimes just calling it like you see it is better than working out a flowery and convoluted metaphor that takes the reader out of the story. The last thing you want is for your reader to stop midsentence and wonder, *Wait. Huh?*

It Happened to Me

I got back the first three chapters of my novel *Me vs. Me* with this note from Farrin: "You have seven similes in nine pages. Don't do that. Vary your techniques and language so it's less obvious that you're using a device."

I don't do that! I thought. *Do I?* I scanned the pages in search of my so-called excessive similes: "Cam was blinking furiously like dirt was caught in his contacts." "My lips were swollen and sticky like I'd spent the day licking envelopes . . ."

Whoops. I guess I do.

Farrin recommended cutting a few, varying the construction of others, and leaving some as is.

And now my prose is smooth. Smooth like freshly waxed legs.—*SM*

A Note about Brand Names and Pop Culture References

Although they are by no means a requirement, brand names and pop culture references in chick lit can be useful. They can give your book the context it needs. For example, part of Cara Lockwood's *Dixieland Sushi* is set in the '80s, so she used brand-name '80s references to orient her reader.

So feel free to drop designer names in your novel if it truly suits your character or story, but be wary of how you use them. And don't rely on them as a substitute for description or personality. "They represent a set of values that lets the writer convey certain characteristics with a minimum of fuss," says Lynn Messina, who used them sparingly but effectively in her fashion-mag satire, *Fashionistas*. "But at the same time, they're also shorthand and lazy—and if your character is nothing but a collection of brand names, then she's not really a character but a billboard."

A lot of writers think these references are a requirement for the genre—if a book doesn't reference Manolo Blahnik, it can't be chick lit, right? (Wrong.) But these elements might also date your novel. Someone who picks up your book five years from now might think Ugg boots and Cosmos are passé and might write your book off as passé, too.

It Happened to Me

In my short story "Know It All" (written for the 2004 U.S. edition of the chick lit anthology *Girls' Night In*), my main character mentions that she feels more passion for Tom Cruise than she does for the ex-boyfriend she's still involved with. In mid-

July 2005, when I was editing the same story for the Australian edition, Tom had undergone a bit of an image change, and I decided that I should choose a movie star with fewer issues, so readers wouldn't think my character was drawn to an over-the-top Scientologist couch jumper. I settled on Jude Law and sent the revised story off to the Australian editor, pleased with my change. Until the next morning, when I read the gossip head-lines. Jude, it seems, had been cheating on his fiancée with his children's nanny. I'd traded in an alleged freak for a reported cad! Sigh. For the UK edition, I changed it to George Clooney. If he goes loco on us, I'm going to feel a little responsible.—*SM*

So what should you do? You should consider why you're adding brand names and pop culture references. If it's because you think it truly suits your novel, great. If you're doing it because you think it isn't chick lit without these references, reconsider. Just because your narrator aspires to step out in Manolos and Chloe jeans doesn't mean she's a shoo-in to be the next chick lit superstar.

NINE

Putting It All Together: The Big Pieces of Your Puzzle

✳ ✳ ✳

As Valerie Frankel, whose *Smart vs. Pretty* was an early chick lit hit, eloquently puts it, "I see a novel as a puzzle I have to figure out, page by page, piece by piece." We couldn't have said it better ourselves (but we will elaborate on it, because that's what we're here for).

Writing a novel is like creating your very own jigsaw puzzle—there are a lot of pieces, and you need to fit them all together just so to create a complete (and, we hope, compelling) image. In puzzles, there are "gateway pieces." No, it's not that the pieces lead to stronger stuff (although puzzles and games can be addictive); it's that once they're in place, everything around them suddenly makes sense, you're filling in blanks in rapid succession, and the picture is starting to look whole. Well, in a novel, there are also hundreds of pieces to fit together, but your puzzle could never be completed without the gateway pieces: story, setting, conflict, plot, and characters.

Story

Back in the day (lo, those four or five years ago), girl gets dumped by boy, loses job, and gets kicked out of apartment; girl gets better boy, finds new job, and scores kick-ass new apartment would have sufficed as far as plot goes. Even the similarly straightforward small-town girl moves to big city, finds boy/job/apartment, then somehow loses one or all would have made publishers atwitter with expectations. Not so anymore. These days, your story actually has to have a hook—something editors can easily pitch to their bosses. Sure, there are authors who can stand out simply by creating a strong voice and a unique character, but a killer story can take anyone a long way.

This is not to say you need to come up with some outlandish, convoluted setup, but you do need to produce something that feels fresh and original—and that you can explain in only a few sentences (which will come in handy when you're writing those query letters we talk about in chapter 13). Maybe a unique twist on the tried-and-true is all you need, like Jennifer Weiner's *Good in Bed*. Weiner started with the girl-gets-dumped premise and raised the stakes: girl gets dumped by guy who then writes about her in a column called "Loving a Larger Woman" in a national magazine? Ouch, but what a fantastic way to exploit a basic chick lit premise.

**CHICK LIT MAD LIBS:
A BEEN THERE, DONE THAT STORY IDEA**

_____-year-old _____, an aspiring _____,
[number]   [woman's first and last name]   [profession]
never expected to find herself _____—not to mention
                                [state of existence]
_____. But ever since she _____, her life has been
[state of existence]   [action]
_____. She can't _____ it on her own, so she'll have to enlist the help
[adjective]   [verb]
of _____, her _____
   [name]   [gay best friend/straight male best friend who's secretly in love
_____
with her/roommate who also happens to be her best friend/recently widowed
_____ to get her out of this _____. With a little bit of
[parent/fill in your own]   [noun]
_____ and a lot of _____, together they'll _____ and _____, and they'll
[noun]   [noun]   [verb]   [verb]
_____ _____ doing it. But when _____ strikes, will_____ be
[verb] [adverb]   [noun]   [same woman]
able to _____ on her own?
        [verb]

What's Your Book About?

Your story and what your novel is about aren't necessarily the same thing. Think about how you might explain each to see the difference. Describing the former: *Oh, well, this woman who's always been a good girl sleeps with her best friend's fiancé, falls in love, and carries on an affair with him leading up to the wedding day.* Describing the latter: *It's a story about love and friendship and how complicated both can be.* The first explanation tells us what happens in Emily Giffin's *Something Borrowed*; the second explains (in Giffin's own words) what the novel is about.

Most chick lit involves some type of self-discovery or self-acceptance, but there can also be a more specific theme underlying it all. In *Good Grief*, the young narrator is coping with the death of her husband, so while self-discovery figures into her journey, the novel also portrays resilience in the face of unexpected loss. In *The Dirty Girls Social Club*, Alisa Valdes-Rodriguez follows a year in the life of six friends, detailing, among other things, their work woes and love troubles, but the book is also about prejudice and friendship and self-respect. Think of some of your favorite chick lit stories and consider what they're about.

Although you want to be mindful of themes and big ideas and perhaps even morals, try not to let them override your story. You need them to give your character a place to grow, to give your story an arc, to bind the characters and scenes and action and dialogue, but it should be subtle, otherwise you risk hitting your reader over the head with your agenda. Your reader doesn't want to be preached at. If she wanted to hear from Dr. Phil, she would have picked up one of his books instead.

Setting

For the sake of believability, you have to work on setting and all the attendant logistics. This means New York, Chicago, Springfield, or whatever locale you choose for your story, but it also means your character's life and background. It's one thing to decide to center your story around, for example, the days and nights of a casting director in Los Angeles; it's another thing to know what those days and nights might truly involve if you are not in fact a casting director in Los Angeles.

If you're a real estate agent in New York writing about being a real estate agent in New York, then you're off and running. Otherwise, to keep it real (literally), you might have to do some research. Don't panic; this kind of research will likely be fun and interesting. It could involve anything from reading up on a certain hobby (*Macrame for Dummies!*) to traveling to a specific place so you can describe it properly to interviewing someone about the ins and outs of her or his job. And if it makes you feel any better, everyone's doing it, even Marian Keyes. "My early novels required little research, as the characters led lives similar to mine," she says. "But for *Angels*, for example, I went to live in L.A. for a while and talked to people in the film business. And for *Anybody Out There?* I had interviews with a number of beauty PR people in London and New York."*

How much emphasis to place on these details depends on how important you want them to be to your story. In *The Nanny Diaries* and *The Devil Wears Prada*, the protagonists' jobs are practically characters themselves. And look at Candace Bushnell's *Sex and the City*: New York is most definitely a character. Almost as vital as Mr. Big.

Conflict

Let's say what you really want to write is a breakup story, but you're not sure about the specifics. How will you make it interesting and unique? How will you make it stand apart from all the other breakup stories? Maybe having just gone through one, you're fascinated by

---

*Just remember to use research as a tool, not as an excuse, OK? If two years down the road you claim, "I can't start writing yet, I'm still researching!" we're going to send you back to chapter 5 without dessert.

the mechanics of it: Who gets to keep the common friends and shared purchases? What happens if one member of the couple was really close with the other's parents or siblings? What if the couple was living together?

You can turn these questions into problems your characters encounter, also known as external conflicts, which will drive your novel forward and help to differentiate your breakup novel from the pack of others. So maybe your heroine has been living with her boyfriend for years and all of a sudden he says he doesn't want to be in a relationship anymore. He gives her an explanation of changing and growing apart and she takes him at his word. But then what? Does she decide she can't be in contact with him anymore because she's so heartbroken? What if he can't get out of the apartment for at least two weeks? Maybe during these two weeks he gives her some false hope.

If you haven't already, you also have to consider who your character is and what else is going on in her life:

⁕ Was this her first long-term relationship? Or was her ex the latest in a long string of live-in boyfriends?

⁕ Does she fall in love too easily or not easily enough?

⁕ Is she flailing at work, or doing better than ever?

⁕ Are her friends being supportive?

⁕ Is there one friend in particular she starts to rely on?

⁕ Imagine the possibility that the friend had been having an affair with the boyfriend and your heroine discovers it. Then your breakup story is one that explores all kinds of betrayals and becomes layered and more interesting.

Along with the external conflicts, you need to consider your characters' internal conflicts, as your novel will depend on a combination of both. "I need the internal conflict to understand the character, so that she has somewhere to grow," says Melissa Senate, whose book *The Breakup Club* added a unique twist to the typical busted-relationship story, "and I need the external conflict for plot, to give the character something interesting to do while she's being poked at by those growing pains." Although we can break them apart and analyze them separately, the two elements are interconnected, and you simply can't have a good novel without both.

If you have trouble understanding the difference, you can think of it this way: External conflict involves something your character does (or that's done to your character), and internal conflict is something she thinks or feels (which, in all likelihood, stems from something that she did or had done to her in the past). So, in Senate's first novel, *See Jane Date*, an external conflict is that Jane needs to find a date for a wedding because she told a little white lie about a hot boyfriend to her family and high school nemesis. But internally, Senate explains, "Jane is struggling with all the insecurities that led her to tell that lie in the first place, like why does she care so much what people think of her?"

In most cases, the external and internal conflicts will collide at some point. It could be that something external happens at the beginning of your novel that forces your character to deal with what's going on inside of her. For example, on page 1 she loses her job. On page 2, she's cycling through all of her feelings of worthlessness and ineptitude. It's the external conflict that will often force your character to deal with the internal conflict.

THE WALL OF CONFLICTS

If you've ever watched a soccer game, you've probably seen that part where one person gets a free kick, which isn't all that free, considering members of the opposite team get to form a wall in front of the goal to try to block the kick and offer distraction. Well, that's sort of like what conflicts are in a novel—they're what's standing in the way of the narrator's happy ending. Of course, the kicker in the game has not only those people and the goalie standing in her way (representing, for our purposes, the external conflict), but also all of her own issues to contend with (internal conflicts). Maybe she's missed her last three free kicks and is convinced she'll miss this one, too. Maybe it's the game point—if she misses, her team will lose the championship—and the pressure is too much for her to handle. All sorts of thoughts and past experiences could be causing her to stand in her own way.

So, once upon a time lived a girl named Brandi. All she wanted was to be a photographer. She wasn't asking for fame and fortune, she just wanted to make a living doing what she loved. But she had massive debt from school and life and buying what little photography equipment she had, so she couldn't afford to quit her job and devote herself full-time to her art. She also had a judgmental live-in boyfriend who was in medical school, so she needed to be able to make enough money for the both of them. These were all obstacles to her goal. In addition, Brandi suffered from extreme self-doubt, as she had grown up in the shadow of her "perfect" older sister and never felt she was very good at anything. She worried that devoting herself to photography would be foolish. Here's what Brandi's Wall of Conflict would look like:

117

CONFLICT IS GOOD

* Once you have an idea for a story or character, brainstorm what the conflicts will be and write everything down. This will help you flesh out both your story and your characters and might ultimately form the basis of a solid outline.

* Don't hold anything back at this phase, just put everything down, no matter how silly it seems. This is for your eyes only, and four bad ideas could lead to one really good one.

Once you separate the wheat from the chaff, you might find you have enough good ideas to hang your novel on.

Of course, after you've identified the problems you plan to throw in your characters' ways, you need to make sure they jibe with what you've already created. You can keep asking yourself questions and trying out scenarios until all the problems fit your story and characters, and soon enough you'll have a serviceable plot. But just remember that the obstacles you create must make sense in the world of your novel. And every single turn should advance the plot or contribute to the reader's understanding of your characters in some way.

Plot

So you have your story idea. You've brainstormed the conflicts. Now you're starting to think about plot. But what's the difference between story and plot? A story is what happens in your book. A plot is how those events are connected: the why and how one event leads to the next. Back to Emily Giffin's story: *This woman who's always been a good girl sleeps with her best friend's fiancé, falls in love, and carries on an affair with him leading up to the wedding day.* If you're thinking about plot, you're thinking along these lines:

* How long has the woman known her best friend's fiancé?
* What causes her to sleep with him? Is it just sex? Is it for revenge?
* What leads her to keep the affair going? Insecurity? Love?
* How does she keep the affair a secret from her friend? Does she flat-out lie? Avoid the friend so she doesn't have to lie?
* Does she consider ending the affair? Does the thought of ending it never cross her mind?

Every question you ask and answer will help you get closer to a solid plot.

Remember when you're piecing together your plot that it needs to feel genuine. One thing should lead to another in a natural and believable way. You've likely started out with an idea for a story or a character (later we'll give you more on which should come first), and as you explore this idea further, a plot will start to form. Sophie Kinsella, whose *Confessions of a Shopaholic* spawned a series of novels, never starts writing until she feels she has a solid sense of what will happen in her story. "I plot endlessly," she says. "That's not to say the plot might not change as I'm writing it, though. And I often end up with a different ending from the one I originally planned." Kinsella never just follows her blueprint blindly, and neither should you. You can't force your characters to do or say things just to service the plot. (Well, you can, but it'll only end in heartbreak for you, since your book won't be as solid as it could be.)

Words of Wisdom

"We have defined a story as a narrative of events arranged in their time-sequence. A plot is also a narrative of events, the emphasis falling on causality. "The king died, and then the queen died" is a story. "The king died, and then the queen died of grief" is a plot. The time sequence is preserved, but the sense of causality overshadows it."—*Aspects of the Novel*, by E. M. Forster

Where Do You Begin?
Characters, Story, or Plot?

It's no surprise how vital your characters are to your book—that's why they got their own chapters in this one. But your story and plot are also important. "What is character but the determination of incident?" asked novelist Henry James. "What is incident but the illustration of character?" In other words, they inform each other. So what should you focus on initially?

Unfortunately, like so much else, there isn't One Right Way, but it's virtually impossible to develop a plot without knowing a little bit about who your characters are. When she sat down to write *Something Borrowed*, all Emily Giffin knew for sure was the basic character and her general story: a good girl who falls in love with her best friend's fiancé. Because Giffin likes to start with the characters and work from there, she listens to them to tell her what the plot would be. "I then build relationships around the main characters. Friendships and romances. And those relationships drive the plot from beginning to end." Caren Lissner started with an image of a particular type of personality for her debut novel and no plot to speak of. "When I started writing *Carrie Pilby*, I just wanted to rant in the voice of a character who was intellectually, but not socially, aware. I made it funny, and she was a unique character, but I wasn't sure exactly what would happen."

Your plot, story, and main character will become so closely entwined that eventually it won't matter which came first; they'll develop and change along with each other the more you get comfortable with each. And soon the pieces of your puzzle will work together to look like a complete picture.

IT'S AS EASY AS 1, 2, 3

All of the preceding information can be summarized into three basic steps that will start you on your way:

1. Come up with a general story idea. This could be as simple as a one-line description.
2. Decide who your main characters are.
3. Brainstorm conflicts (internal and external) to come up with your plot.

The Cherry on Top: Your Title

Another important piece of your puzzle is the name of your book. Maybe the title was what inspired the novel. Maybe you're already on page 200 and you're still calling it "the book." The advantage to a killer title is that it can get you a leg up with agents—they're more likely to take a look at your stuff if your title knocks their socks off. If your manuscript is called *Good in Bed* or *The Devil Wears Prada*, an agent is going to take a long look.

Back in 2004, Kristin Harmel wanted to write a novel about a journalist who everyone thinks is having an affair with a movie star. "I knew that having a catchy title, especially for a debut novel, could make all the difference in the world," she says. After thinking about it constantly, but before she started writing, Kristin finally came up with her killer title, *How to Sleep with a Movie Star*, one night when she was tossing and turning in bed.

If you've polled your friends, family, neighbors, and random people you meet on the subway and still can't find the perfect title, don't despair. Once you get an agent and a publisher, they'll likely come to your rescue. Melissa Senate's first novel started out as *The Flirt Night Roundtable* before the publisher changed it to *See Jane Date*. Emily Giffin's *Something Borrowed* was once *Rolling the Dice*. Closer to home, *Monkey Business* was *Poacher*, and *Me vs. Me* was *Going Both Ways*. This book was *Like Life but Funnier*.

Spend time thinking about it—but spend more time making your writing sparkle. A good title will get you in the door. The rest of the manuscript will get you a book deal.

TEN

Keeping It All Together: Structure and Pacing

✳ ✳ ✳

When you're doing all the work discussed in the previous chapter, keep in mind that a story needs structure—a beginning, middle, and end—as well as a good pace. That might sound obvious, but you'd be surprised how easy it is to forget pretty much everything when you're mired in pages of writing and piles of Post-Its. Your book couldn't exist without the plot and characters, but structure is the stuff that keeps it all together.

Beginnings

Now that you know what you want to write about, it's time to get started.

> It was a dark and . . .
> It was a bright and sunny . . .
> I was on my way home when . . .
> On my way home, I . . .
> I . . .

Hmm. Where do you begin?

Think about your opening as the first impression. You want it to be dynamic, right? You want to charm your reader in some way. More often than not, you'll perfect this crucial piece of your puzzle when you revise (which, conveniently, we discuss in chapter 12), and you shouldn't worry about getting it just so until after you know exactly what you want for your book.

Let's pretend you've already completed the first draft, and you're revising. You want to have the best damn beginning your book can have. Because if the girl in the bookstore likes your title/jacket/back cover enough to flip open your book, she'd better get reeled right in with that first line or paragraph.

Here are some opening lines that got—and kept—our attention:

> The second time Ian Dunne came into my life, I
> was trapped under a pile of bodies, behind a sheet
> of plate glass.—*Hand-Me-Down*, by Lee Nichols

How can I be a widow? Widows wear horn-rimmed glasses and cardigan sweaters that smell like mothballs and have crepe-paper skin and names like Gladys or Midge and meet with their other widow friends once a week to play pinochle.—*Good Grief*, by Lolly Winston

I WILL: Stop Smoking. Drink no more than fourteen alcohol units per week. Reduce circumference of thighs by 3 inches (1½ inches each) . . . —*Bridget Jones's Diary*, by Helen Fielding

All three openings set the tone for the book that follows. They also manage to orient the reader—they tell you the point of view and a little about the main character. *Hand-Me-Down* places you smack in the middle of the story, forcing you to wonder who this Ian Dunne character is. And when the narrator met him the first time. And why in the world was she under a pile of bodies? *Good Grief*'s opening tells you that this narrator, this book, is not going to be about what you expect, since the protagonist is not a "typical" widow. And anyway, what happened to her husband? Finally, there's the *Bridget Jones* quote, which makes the reader laugh. But more than that, it speaks to the Everywoman. It draws the reader in because she immediately relates to the protagonist. She, too, wants to quit smoking/stop boozing/lose weight. If she sees herself in your book, she's not going to put it back on the shelf, is she? Oh no, she's taking it straight to the cash register.

Once you draw your reader in with your opening, you still have major work to do: Not only do you need to set the stage by identifying your character and giving a sense of place, setting, and time, but you should also introduce the story. You don't want to bombard your reader with too much information, but at the same time you don't want to leave her stranded without a clue. It's a fine balance, and one you have to work at to get just right.

Let's say you're writing about a girl who finds her boyfriend in bed with a neighbor and then has nowhere to live but in the stockroom of the boutique where she works. Where should the story start?

* When she walks in on the boyfriend?
* When she moves into the stockroom?
* When she first meets the boyfriend?
* Before she meets the boyfriend? When she gets the job at the boutique?

There is no one right answer here. But whatever choice you make—whether you start in the thick of things, before, or after—will shape your story in a particular way.

In *The Undomestic Goddess*, Sophie Kinsella tells the story of a workaholic attorney who, after making a massive mistake at her London law firm, ends up working as a housekeeper in the suburbs. Kinsella could start the book in many places. During the meltdown. Once she starts work as a housekeeper. But in the opening scene, we see Samantha Sweeting clearly being her workaholic self, having smuggled in both her Blackberry and cell phone to her spa's "Ultimate De-stress Experience." Only on page 45 does Samantha make the mistake that leads to the meltdown. Kinsella chose to establish Samantha's natural tendencies before getting things going. Since the book is about her transformation, the story wouldn't be as effective if Kinsella had started with the meltdown. We might not care if we weren't already familiar with Samantha's character.

Jennifer Weiner's *Good in Bed*, the story of how a woman's life changes after her ex-boyfriend writes about her in a national magazine, begins right in the middle of the action. By the second page, Cannie Shapiro has seen the article "Loving a Larger Woman."

By launching her book with the life-changing moment, Weiner is throwing her reader right into the deep end—and giving her plenty of reasons for not wanting to get out of the pool. Could she have started the novel with the breakup? Probably. But the story is less about the breakup and more about how Cannie deals with the aftermath. Weiner effectively flashes back to their first meeting and breakup without losing the flow of the current story.

Lee Nichols opens *Tales of a Drama Queen* with a letter addressed to Elle Medina that tells us something big has already happened. The narration begins with Elle fleeing Washington, D.C., because her ex-fiancé has gone off and married someone else. We don't see them together as a couple, we don't see her moving out, we just see her absconding with his prized stamp collection, getting drunk on the plane, and spilling her guts to the (uninterested) person in the seat beside her as she heads for her best friend's couch in California. A perfectly fitting scene for a drama queen.

CHICK LIT MAD LIBS: BAD FIRST PAGE

I'm not sure I've heard my boss of _____ years correctly, so I ask
                                    [number]
him to repeat himself.

"I said, 'You're fired,'" he says.

"Oh," I say _____, nervously pulling at the sleeve of my _____
[adverb]   _[color]_
_____ blouse. "I thought that's what you said."
[brand-name]

Less than _____ minutes later, I'm at my _____ -cloth-walled
           [number]   _[color]_
cubicle, stuffing _____ into a cardboard box when my
                  [specific office supplies]
best friend and coworker, _____, peeks over the fake wall we
                                  [woman's name]
share.

"He didn't!" she exclaims.

"He did," I mumble quietly.

"Oh, _____ , it'll be OK."
     [another woman's name]

I pull down my little velcroed-to-the-wall mirror and catch sight
of myself in it—_____ eyes all puffy and red, _____ _____ hair look-
             [color]   _[adjective] [color]_
ing messy as usual, and _____ _____. I sniffle _____ and
                         [adjective] [facial feature]   _[adverb]_
toss the mirror into the box, where it lands _____ atop a photo booth
                                          [adverb]
picture of me and my loving and supportive boyfriend of _____
                                                [number]
years, _____, who I just
     [man's name, one that ends in -ad, like Brad or Chad or Tad]
know is going to propose to me tonight, since he's been acting weird
all week.

"How do you know, _____?" I inquire.
                  [first woman's name]

"Because, _____, I've known you since _____th
         [second woman's name]   _[number]_
grade, when we met in Mr. _____'s _____ class because we
                          [surname] _[school subject]_
were seated alphabetically and your last name is _____ and
                                        [another surname]
my last name is _____
                 _[a third surname that begins with the same letter as the sec-
_____ and you were the class clown and I was always shy . . .
ond surname]

Storytelling Devices

How you choose to tell your story will definitely inform your structure. You could go for straightforward or clever, depending on what suits your idea and your style. Some of the best chick lit novels follow a traditional narrative structure, while others use a gimmick or hook to good effect. *Bridget Jones's Diary*, for example, is, naturally, in diary format, so it's a (nearly) day-by-day account of a year in Bridget's life. The chapters in *Good Grief* delineate the stages of grief one must go through (some real, some made up by the author). In Sarah Salway's debut, *The ABCs of Love*, she breaks down her chapters alphabetically, from "Ambition" to "Zzzz."

If you're going to go the unconventional route, just make sure the device suits your story. If you want to include lists at the start of each chapter, for example, don't just jam them in there and call it innovative. Make the lists a part of the story, a habit of the character—something that makes it feel natural and not contrived. Any device you choose should help deliver the story; it should never impede it or overshadow it.

The Scene

When you get down to basics, your book is made up of scenes. One after the other. Opening scene, middle scenes, ending scene. Sometimes a chapter is a single scene, sometimes it's made up of a few connected scenes. You already know why the opening scene is important. But remember that *every* scene is important.

Each scene serves a purpose. You can't (well you can, but you shouldn't) write (or, more importantly, keep) a scene for no reason. Laura Caldwell, who writes both chick lit (*The Night I Got Lucky*) and mysteries (*Look Closely*), always asks herself, "What exactly is this scene doing for the novel? It can't just be a scene about shopping for a ball gown simply because you, the author, shopped for a ball gown last week and thought it was fun. The scene has to show the tension between the two friends shopping together, or it has to force them to run into the ex-boyfriend your protagonist can't forget. Every damn scene has to advance the novel in some way. If it's not moving the novel forward, it has to be cut, no matter how fabulous the ball gowns or how witty the dialogue was while trying them on."

The purpose of the scene is to do one or more of the following:

* Introduce a character.
* Create setting or context.
* Move the plot forward.
* Show character growth.
* Develop the relationships between characters.
* Give information to the reader that's necessary for understanding the character (i.e., backstory—what happened to the character before the beginning of the book).
* Give information to the reader that's necessary for following the plot.
* Create suspense (and not in the horror movie way—in the subtle, what-happens-next way).

No matter how funny that scene you just wrote is, if it doesn't serve one of the above purposes, it has to go. Usually, the scenes that serve multiple purposes are the strongest.

If you're wondering how to organize a scene, think of a scene as a microcosm of a novel. Each should feel complete and have a beginning, middle, and end. Say these are the linear events that must take place in your scene:

A: Jane's boss lets her off work early.

B: Jane drives home.

C: Jane walks into her apartment.

D: Jane finds her boyfriend on the kitchen table having sex with her neighbor.

You can write this scene in a few different ways:

1. Start at the beginning, and tell the story A, B, C, D. In other words, you'd start the scene with something like this:

   > **"You did a great job today, Jane, why don't you take the afternoon off?" my boss said.**

2. Start in the middle, with B or C, and refer to A (or not, if it's boring or obvious). This would look something like this:

   > **I heard a clang as I unlocked the door. I hoped the cat hadn't broken another vase.**

3. Mention or foreshadow the end, and then go back to the beginning. Which would look like this:

   > **I never expected to be the kind of woman who walked in on her boyfriend having sex with the neighbor on her kitchen table. But when my boss**

sent me home early, that's exactly what I became.

"You did a great job today, Jane, why don't
you take the afternoon off?" my boss said.

MAKING THE SCENE

Take a scene you've already written, or use a scene from your favorite book. Break the scene up into three to five sections (A–E), depending on what happens in the scene. Now play around with the order: If the scene started at the beginning, try starting it at the middle of the action. See how it changes the feel of the scene.

Pacing

Remember the old adage (well, it hasn't quite made it to old adage status, but we're crossing our fingers), *Just because it happened to you doesn't mean you should put it in your novel?* That applies here as well. If your novel is merely a string of anecdotes and interactions with little to bind them together, there's really nothing for a reader to grab onto that will keep her reading. You don't want your novel to plod along; you want it to gallop in some places and linger in others. You want to luxuriate in some scenes and march through others.

How can you work on this? By making strong transitions, trimming the excess fat in your scenes, getting rid of scenes that don't either move the story along or contribute to your characters' development, tightening your writing (refer to chapter 12), varying the settings of your scenes (your book is not a sitcom—the whole story does not have to take place at either Central Perk or Rachel's apartment), varying the lengths of your scenes, and creating little mini mysteries within your story.

It Happened to Me

In her revision letter for *Frogs & French Kisses* (my second teen chick lit novel about a witch), my editor told me that I had a lot of scenes of the two sisters sitting in their room talking about using magic and hardly any scenes showing them using magic. Her recommendation was to "get Miri out in the field" in order to vary the Miri scenes in the book. While before, the exchanges were a little boring (but necessary for character development), moving them to a unique location (they weren't just talking about helping orphans in Africa—they actually zapped themselves over to Tanzania) helped the scenes pop.—*SM*

Some writers consider their pacing as they write, and others don't at all. "I'm aware of pace in a musical sense," says Alisa Valdes-Rodriguez (*Playing with Boys*), who has a background in music. "In jazz, solos are paced with starts, middles, and ends, and I follow that sensibility when I write words, too. My sentences, too, tend to be short enough to be read in one breath. That's because I'm a sax player. After decades of blowing a wind instrument, I naturally think in short bursts. So, in that sense, I have micropacing that is short, almost choppy, and macropacing that is structured like a song, or suite, or symphony." But Lynda Curnyn (*Bombshell*) doesn't dwell on pacing when she's working on a first draft. "If I'm flowing," says Curnyn, "generally the pace is good. But I do go back later to tighten things, especially in the beginning."

Words of Wisdom

"Novels are narratives, and narrative, whatever its medium—words, film, strip-cartoon—holds the interest of an audience by raising questions in their minds, and delaying the answers."—*The Art of Fiction*, by David Lodge

Regardless of whether you're conscious of your pacing, something to ask yourself as you write (or as you revise) is, *Will my reader be compelled to keep turning the pages?* The answer will be yes if you've given her something to look forward to on a page-by-page or scene-by-scene level—an answer to a question, a solution to a problem, a clue to a puzzle. In the big picture of your book, it might be, *Will she get the job/guy/personal satisfaction she's angling for?* But in this smaller sense it's, *Will her presentation at the big meeting go smoothly? Will the guy who's fifteen minutes late to the bar actually stand her up? Will she embarrass herself or achieve her goal by putting the moves on her office crush?*

When you're plotting out your scenes, piecing together your puzzle, consider what keeps you reading when you're engrossed in a novel: It's that feeling of wanting to know what comes next. It's as if a book has a hundred little stories beneath the surface of the main one. Caldwell is certainly conscious of this as she writes. "I try to have a 'Whoa!' ending to each and every scene and chapter. It's impossible all the time, of course, but I try to write a scene or chapter ending and ask myself, 'If I was a reader, would I absolutely have to keep reading here, or could I turn off my light and go to bed?' If the scene has dragged on and settled gently to a halt, that's no good. I'll sometimes cut whole pages of a scene and try to go back and end on a high point."

Whether you work on it as you write or think about it while you revise, just promise us that at some point in your writing process you'll give pacing your attention.

PICK UP THE PACE

* Next time you're reading a novel, mark the places in the story where you want to or do stop reading.

* Afterward, look over all of your markings to get a sense of what makes a reader lose interest. Perhaps it's a scene that drags on too long, dialogue that goes nowhere, or descriptions more boring than your fourth-grade math teacher. There's no need to be consciously critical—just make note of your flagging interest level.

* Learn from these authors' mistakes; in your revision stage, you can apply the same exercise to your own manuscript and avoid some of the more common pacing pitfalls.

Endings

What's a chick lit writer to do? You want your heroine to be happy, but should you give her everything her heart desires? You need to wrap everything up, but you don't want to rush it, and you don't want it to drag on forever. There's no rule that says you must start your ending seven pages from the last one or that your heroine must have a ring on her finger and every single problem solved by the time you type the final word. There's no checklist of Things to Do to End Your Novel. Your ending, like everything else, should fit the book and feel natural and all that good stuff. But you should address all of the questions you've planted along the way (and for the love of God, don't introduce a new story line in the last chapter unless you're consciously paving the way for a sequel).

Mistakes I've Known

Of course you want to wrap everything up nicely, give your characters if not a traditional happy ending, then at least an upbeat conclusion, but watch out for the improbable, too-neat, hit-and-run ending. I call it the "hospital corner ending." The one where everyone ever mentioned in the book gets exactly what he or she wants (or deserves), and it all happens in five pages or less. Life is messy; I don't want to read a fictionalized version of it that's impossibly neat.—*FJ*

If the classic happily-ever-after doesn't suit your novel (which is totally OK, despite what you might have heard), your ending should at the very least be positive and hopeful. The key to a good chick lit ending is that the character has reevaluated her life and has grown in some distinct way. She's most likely in a good place and looking forward to the future. She might have a guy beside her or a fabulous new job, or maybe just the promise of a guy or a fabulous new job. She's definitely happier with herself. The key is, although you want your reader to be sad about leaving your characters behind, you want her to close your book with a smile on her face.

Eleven

Grammar and Punctuation Are Hot: More Elements of Style

✻ ✻ ✻

You're a genius. Your story is brilliant. Every line you write is like a shiny diamond with the perfect combination of cut, color, and clarity. Fantastic. But if you don't have a basic grasp of grammar, punctuation, spelling, and word usage, then none of that matters, because your reader might be so appalled, she'll feel no remorse in putting your manuscript in the reject pile after perusing only the first few pages. The occasional typo here and there is fine. Everyone makes mistakes. Most of this is stuff you can worry about when you're revising (see chapter 12). But if you turn in a manuscript that is sloppy and suggests you're lazy, you just might turn off an agent or editor.

That said, this book isn't a style guide. We will not be presenting you with an extensive course on the mechanics of writing. There are books for that which you should absolutely go out and buy. (At the very least, go pick up *The Elements of Style*. It's small and cute and surprisingly exhaustive.) We will, however, offer up some mistakes you can easily avoid.* So, pay attention, please.

---

*Think of this chapter as "Farrin's Pet Peeves." That's how we're thinking of it. Ah, sweet justice!—FJ

Common Mistakes

You'd be surprised how easy it is to make a mistake in your manuscript. You might think that technology can save you; after all, you have spell check and grammar check—what could possibly go wrong?

Soundalikes

You know how sometimes, if you don't know the words to a song, you just kind of make up something that sounds vaguely like what you *think* you hear? Well, occasionally you do that in your writing, and you might not even be aware of it. In many cases you're using a real word, so you can't rely on spell check to point it out to you.

Here are some common soundalikes you might misuse in your chick lit manuscript.

affect/effect

Don't you hate how your nemesis *affects* you? Don't you wish you could *effect* some kind of change in this relationship? Or, at the very least, don't you wish you had the same *effect* on her?

dessert/desert

This one is more often than not a simple typo. Mmm, *dessert*.

jive/jibe

A lot of people write *jive* when they mean *jibe*. Let's say the sentence is "His actions didn't j—— with what I'd heard about him." What would you write? If you said *jibe*, pat yourself on the back. Chances are you'll never use *jive* as a verb.

loathe/loath

You *loathe* the smarmy guy who sits in the cubicle next to yours; but you are *loath* to tell your boss about it, since he's the boss's son.

loose/lose

Another common typo that comes from being a little *loose* with the keyboard. Don't *lose* your head over it.

than/then

When you're comparing things, always use *than*. "My shoes are way cuter *than* hers." If you remember that simple rule, *then* you'll be sure to always get these two right.

Homophones

Some words sound exactly alike but are spelled differently and don't mean even close to the same thing.

Here are some common homophones you might misuse in your chick lit manuscript.

bear/bare

He's a neat freak. He couldn't *bear* to watch you walking on the dirty sidewalk in your *bare* feet.

compliment/complement

She meant to *compliment* her boss when she told her the silver in her hair *complements* the metallic in her dress.

faze/phase

Nothing *fazes* her these days. She's in one of her totally accepting *phases*.

heels/heals

Her three-inch Marc Jacobs *heels* looked good, but they weren't going to *heal* her broken heart.

it's/its

It's is the contraction of *it* and *is*. And it's often confused with the adjective *its*, its homophone.

past/passed

In the *past* he always *passed* her on the way to work. One's a noun, the other is the past tense of a verb. Got it?

peek/peak/pique

When she got to the top of the mountain, she took a *peek* beyond the *peak*. What she saw really *piqued* her interest.

pore/pour

She *pored* over his love letter after she *poured* herself a glass of wine.

while/wile

You might be *whiling* away your time, but at least you're using your feminine *wiles*.

you're/your

This one is like *it's* and *its*. *You're* just never sure about *your* spelling on this one, are you?*

grammar

There are only two things nearly everyone gets wrong at some point—dangling participles and misplaced modifiers.

> **Standing there in heels, Roger was at least three inches shorter than me.**

Chances are, unless Roger is a cross-dresser, this is a dangling participle and the sentence should actually look like this:

> **Standing there in heels, I was at least three inches taller than Roger.**

Here's another example:

> **On the rack, I thought it was the most perfect dress ever.**

The speaker in the sentence is not hanging on the rack and is not the subject of this sentence; the dress is. So the sentence should be recast like this:

> **On the rack, it was the most perfect dress I'd ever seen.**

If you're still confused about any of these words, I trust you have a dictionary or access to www.m-w.com. As my mom used to say, "Look it up."—FJ

As for those modifiers, they're pretty easy to misplace:

> She only bought two of the five dresses she
> tried on.

The modifier in this sentence, *only*, refers to the dresses and not the action of buying. So this sentence should look like this:

> She bought only two of the five dresses she
> tried on.

Unless you're specifying that she bought two of the dresses and hid the other three on the sale rack.   .

As for the other rules you might have learned in grammar school, like never split an infinitive and never end a sentence with a preposition, use your best judgment. In some cases, breaking the rule will save you from having an incredibly stiff and awkward sentence. Say the sentence aloud (not *allowed*) and see what sounds best to your ear; sometimes that's all you have to go on. (Unless you think *that's all you have on which to go* sounds better, in which case—well, *never ever* trust your ear.)

General Sloppiness and Other Things Farrin Hates

Oh, I've been waiting for this. Herewith, things that drive me insane when I'm editing. Chances are, they'll drive your potential editor crazy as well.

1. **Misspellings:** As we mentioned earlier, I'm not talking about a typo here and there or the occasional homophone mix-up; I'm

talking about manuscripts riddled with errors. Make sure to read over your work before you send it out to an agent or editor. You're trying to impress them, and having them think you're illiterate is just not impressive.

2. **Inconsistency:** Sometimes writers can't decide which tense to use, so they inadvertently switch back and forth. Sometimes writers forget how they spelled a character's name—was she Kathy or Cathy? Pick one and stick with it. Don't expect your reader to have the patience to compensate for your mistakes.

3. **Misused and misplaced punctuation:** This happens mostly with dialogue. Some writers don't realize that the comma goes inside the quotation marks, or even that it's supposed to be a comma at all. So I see dialogue like this:

> **"Don't do that", she said.**

Or like this:

> **"Don't do that." She said.**

When really it should be:

> **"Don't do that," she said.**

4. **Misplaced dialogue tags:** While we're on the subject of dialogue, keep in mind that in a conversation between Jane and Ethel (they're friends even though they have different reading habits), you shouldn't put Jane's dialogue with Ethel's action. This is incorrect:

"Don't do that," Jane said. Ethel looked at her.

"Why not?" Ethel said.

This is better:

"Don't do that," Jane said.

Ethel looked at her. "Why not?"

5. **Overexclaiming:** I don't have a problem with the occasional exclamation point every once in a while. But when it crops up in every third line of dialogue—then I have a problem! Characters are yelling at each other all over the place and the whole book feels like a shouting match!!!!!! Use the exclamation point sparingly, and it will reward you by being more effective.

6. **One- and two-sentence paragraphs as far as the eye can see:** Short paragraphs are fine once in a while, but if all you have are two-sentence paragraphs, your story will feel stilted. Some of them serve a purpose, but a lot of them can be combined to form a larger, meatier narrative with fewer starts and stops.

7. **Overuse of the word *very*:** I hate the word *very*. I generally mark to delete it unless it adds something in the way of rhythm or meaning, but in most cases it doesn't. When you feel yourself relying on *very*, try letting the adjective it's modifying stand on its own. You might be very surprised to see it does fine without it.

8. **Overuse of vague and imprecise words, like *somehow*.** This is another word I try to erase from the page. The word *somehow* means the writer is being vague; being specific is preferable. In some cases, you can just do away with the word

completely. For example: "Somehow, I managed to get to my feet." The *somehow* is unnecessary. The sentence functions perfectly well without it and even communicates the same meaning: It wasn't easy to get to your feet.

Words of Wisdom

"The surest way to arouse and hold the reader's attention is by being specific, definite, and concrete."—*The Elements of Style*, by William Strunk Jr. and E. B. White

---

9. **Overuse of long hyphenated adjectives:** You've seen them everywhere—they're those long-string-of-words-as-adjective adjectives. Once in a while this is fine. It's one of those styles that's become popular in magazines and commercial fiction. But don't overdo it. And don't do it unless you truly believe it adds something to your sentence, character, or voice. I once read, in a published novel (a successful one), a hyphenated adjective that made me want to throw the book across the room.* You want people to feel passionately about your words, sure, but not quite in that way.

10. **Confusing *that* and *which*:** There is a difference between these words. They are not, as most people seem to believe, interchangeable. Consider these two sentences:

> **She walked into the dressing room that was empty and sat down.**

I know you want to know what the offender was, so I'll paraphrase: "She sauntered across the sprinkled-with-small-children playground to her car."—FJ

She walked into the dressing room, which was
empty, and sat down.

The first sentence suggests there were many dressing rooms to choose from and she walked into the one empty one. *That* in the first sentence is a restrictive pronoun—it identifies which dressing room. In the second sentence, *which* is nonrestrictive, which means it gives information about the specific dressing room in question. The comma usually clues people in so they know to use *which* in the second situation. But writers seem less clear about the first sentence. In the UK, *that* and *which* are interchangeable; in the good ol' U.S. of A., go with *that*. It's the American thing to do.

These are but a few nitpicky style issues. They should not get in the way of writing your novel, but understanding them will help make your prose stronger.

If a lot of the information in this chapter was new to you and you're feeling particularly style-challenged, don't panic. Buy some books that address the mechanics of writing (we can't stress enough how much you'll appreciate *The Elements of Style*), and you'll be fine. Promise.

Twelve

Not So Fast: Revisiting and Revising

❋ ❋ ❋

Yay, you're done! This is fantastic news. Take a deep breath, back away from the computer, maybe call someone to express your glee. Hell, call everyone! Treat yourself to a nice dinner, go buy that purse you've been eyeing, sleep late. Celebrate in whatever way suits you best. You've worked hard, and you deserve a treat.

Now for the less-than-fantastic news: Just because you wrote "The End" doesn't mean your manuscript is done. Of course we're proud of you, and you should be proud of you, too, because finishing a first draft is no easy feat. But there's still a fair amount of work to be done before you're ready to send your masterpiece out to agents or editors. It's called *revising*. (Unless you're lucky enough to have written a pristine first draft, in which case, for your next trick you should try your hand at turning water into wine.) If writing a novel is like a triathlon, revising is the last leg—the run. The end is near, but you still have to work your ass off to get there. So, catch your breath, and maybe refill your water bottle. And, get ready, set, go.

Time Off for Good Behavior

Each author has her own method for revising, but most agree on one thing: You deserve a break. "Breaks from manuscripts are invaluable," says Lee Nichols (*True Lies of a Drama Queen*), who has written a few nonfiction books in addition to her three chick lit novels. "It gives you the chance to forget the characters, plot, and scenes for a couple months and go back to a manuscript with a fresh mind." Not everyone has the luxury of (or the patience for) a couple of months, though. Alisa Valdes-Rodriguez (*Playing with Boys*) waits a few days before she reads it again and starts "scrubbing."

Caren Lissner (*Carrie Pilby*), however, takes another approach: "People will say that you need to put your first draft away for a while, but let's face it: We're writers, and we have egos, and we want to reread what we just wrote and be proud of it." But you should try to ignore your ego in this case. You really should give yourself and your manuscript a rest. You'll both need it.

Cara Lockwood, author of *I Did (But I Wouldn't Now)*, and a self-professed procrastinator, sees the value in squeezing in some downtime. "If I have the time before my deadline (which I usually don't), I'll try to take a few days off from the manuscript to try to get perspective. If I don't have a few days, I'll take a few hours." Sometimes not writing is an important part of the writing process. You need to give yourself the time to relax, recharge, and get ready to revise.

The First Read-Through

Once you've taken a little time away (whether you opted for a few hours or a few weeks), sit yourself back down, roll up your sleeves, and get back to work. You're about to switch hats from writer to editor.

Depending on how you've been writing, this could be the millionth time you've read through your manuscript from the beginning or the first time. It doesn't matter—because now your goal is different. You're no longer writing this story from scratch; you're reshaping and tweaking what's already on the page. What you need to be sensitive to this time around is determining what's not working and how best to fix it.

An effective way to approach this part of the process is to print that baby out and grab your Post-Its and your pen (it doesn't have to be red, unless you desperately need to be reminded of school papers). You might be trying to conserve paper or preserve your million-dollar ink cartridge (or maybe you can't get a free ten minutes with the printer at your day job), but bite the bullet and press Print. It's easier to spot problems on the page than it is on a computer screen. Once you've marked the problem spots, go back to them on-screen and decide what you need to do to fix the problem.

The Kindness of "Strangers"

We trust you and all, but we recommend that you solicit an outside opinion whenever possible. Spouses, critique partners, friends, agents, pen pals—they're virtual strangers to your material, and their input can be invaluable. It isn't easy to critique your own work, which is why it's helpful to have someone whose judgment you trust and who you know will follow through and actually read your draft and give you feedback.

> "I give a copy to my husband to read, because he's pretty smart, and he also will tell me honestly if something isn't working. If I think he's right, then I take his advice, but if I think he's wrong, I can say, 'He's a guy. What does he know?' It's the best of both worlds, really."—Cara Lockwood, author of *I Did (But I Wouldn't Now)*

After she celebrates finishing her first draft, Kristin Gore (*Sammy's Hill*) solicits comments from a select group of people. "I give the draft to my editor and a few trusted readers," she says. "Then I take some time to absorb their suggestions, including those with which I immediately disagree. I've learned that my instant reactions are not necessarily my wisest ones, so I consciously build in absorption time to the feedback portion of my process. I take a short break from the manuscript"—see, everyone lives by The Break!—"and try to return fresher and better-informed for the revision."

Alisa Valdes-Rodriguez says she doesn't understand writers who keep to themselves. "I'm a social girl, trained in newspapers,"

151

she explains. "I need feedback constantly." She gets notes from her agent and editors and then goes right back to work. And for anyone who gets frustrated about not turning out a perfect first draft, take comfort in these words from the *New York Times* bestselling author: "It takes me three or four stabs to get it right."

At this point in your career, it's not likely that you have a team of agents and editors waiting to critique your work, so what should you do? If you're friends (or even acquaintances) with someone else who's working on a novel, you can offer to trade critiques—a sort of "you show me yours, I'll show you mine" situation that works out for both parties. You could also ask a friend whose taste in books you trust. You could ask your mom and dad, but that's probably only going to get you praise, which, while nice, isn't what you need right now. You need someone who'll take a cold, hard look at what you've got and give you some cold, hard feedback.

There are Web sites and online communities that offer critiques for a fee or where you can meet other aspiring chick lit writers who are willing to trade critiques. Check out www.chicklitwriters.com, the chick lit community board on www.eHarlequin.com, and the Yahoo group http://groups.yahoo.com/group/chicklit.

Problem Spots

A lot of problems might be lurking in your first draft; that's why it's also called the *rough* draft, because it's, y'know, *rough*. And now you have an opportunity to smooth it out. As you go through, you'll want to pay attention to issues both large and small. Whether you do one read for the big stuff and another for the small things or you try to catch it all in one fell swoop is up to you. It depends on how you work and what you're capable of. But as you're polishing the pages, here are some problem spots to watch out for:

* **Too much exposition:** Your first chapters could need some tweaking because they're too focused on giving information rather than providing an appealing opening to your story, slowing down the pacing and not giving your reader much impetus to keep turning the pages. You might also find that you've repeated details throughout the manuscript—overexpositioning, as it were. You have to trust that your readers are smart enough to remember that a character you introduced as your protagonist's brother in chapter 3 is still your protagonist's brother in chapter 6.

* **Character inconsistencies:** This could be something as small as a character being blonde on one page and redheaded on another or as big as her personality not being believable throughout.

* **A character with too much character, or maybe not enough:** As you're reading, you might discover that what seemed cute and quirky in a character is annoying and over-the-top. Yes, of course, this is fiction, and you need to step things up a notch, but you don't want your characters to be caricatures. On the flip side, you don't want them to be silhouettes, either. You want them to be well-rounded and convincing. And you want people to want to read about them.

Mistakes I've Known

While I was reading a published author's second manuscript, I found myself not falling in love with her new main character. I'd often held her first book up as an example of perfectly realized characters, so I was surprised by my reaction. This new novel had a brilliant premise, the kind that could hook people with a Hollywood-like one-line pitch. (That is, after all, how I'd been hooked, long before the idea was turned into an actual manuscript.) But it wasn't working for me, and I realized it was because I couldn't feel the main character. She was nondescript, and since this was a first-person account of events in her life, she needed to be, at the very least, interesting. Ideally, she would also be charming and funny and endearing, despite her caustic humor and loner tendencies. So, armed with my comments (and her agent's feedback), the author went through the manuscript page by page, line by line, and found ways to bring out her character more. She did this by replacing humdrum descriptions with more evocative language, showing more interactions between her narrator and her friends and family, and focusing on getting to know her character so that her readers could, too.—*FJ*

⁂ **Language snafus:** Remember all that stuff we talked about in chapter 8? The unintentional repetition of words or phrases, bad dialogue tags, purple prose, an inconsistent tone? This is the time to make the fixes that will make your writing stronger. You want your reader to feel as though the writing was effortless, as if it just flew out of your mouth and onto the page. And to achieve that, you need to put in a lot of effort.

* **Sagging middle:** That urge to put the manuscript down after the first hundred pages? That's the sagging middle, dragging down your story. Diet and exercise won't make it go away—only a nip here and a tuck there will do. This is a pacing problem, and you'll need to figure out what needs cutting or rearranging. If this is your problem, the next section goes out to you, baby.

See the Delete Key, Touch the Delete Key, Love the Delete Key

You're on a desert island with your manuscript and you can choose only one key to bring with you for your revision. What would it be? That's right, the delete key. (Was it the heading of this section that gave it away?) You simply couldn't revise without it. (If you answered "the exclamation point key," please go back and reread chapter 11.)

Once you've determined what your problem areas are, the delete key will figure prominently in your revisions. You will no doubt be adding and rewriting at this stage, but you will be trimming as well. Whether on a line-by-line basis or in a general plot kind of way, this is the time to streamline. Some writers attempt a literary feel and end up overwriting, stuffing their sentences with unnecessary adjectives and adverbs. Others go overboard in making sure their readers understand a particular nuance of their fictional world and end up coming off as pedantic or condescending. Or they fall in love with an image, phrase, or exchange that doesn't really serve much purpose. (A lot of writing teachers refer to these as "little darlings" and will tell you that they need to be killed. They are more often than not totally right. It's futile to resist.) These are tough cuts to make but will ultimately serve your book well.

It could be that an entire subplot needs to go or, as the case was for Cara Lockwood's *Pink Slip Party*, a whole person. "My editor wasn't happy with a secondary character, Cyndi, a friend of the main character, Jane," she recalls somewhat forlornly. "Breaking up with Cyndi was very difficult to do, because I liked Cyndi. She was the ideal friend—sweet, supportive, and completely indecisive about her own life and career, which I can understand because I'm not always the take-charge type. Unfortunately, my editor thought she was too wishy-washy and didn't add enough to the story. After I fumed about this for a few days (*How can she not like Cyndi? I love Cyndi!*), I realized that she was right. Cyndi was taking up room in the book but not adding much to it—sort of like that friend you know who is fun to have around, but who never picks up a round of drinks. Cyndi just wasn't pulling her own weight. So, I had to merge some of the good parts of Cyndi into another character in the book, Steph, Jane's coworker."

Mistakes I've Known

I once received a final manuscript that clocked in at 520 pages. And the font was on the small side. I had bought it based on a proposal, so this page count came as quite the shock to me. (I believe an audible gasp was involved.) Without even cracking it open, though, I knew what needed to be done. I wasn't sure what the specifics would be, but I knew that my first read-through would be with an eye for what was extraneous. It's not as though we in the chick lit world have a strict page limit, but it's pretty safe to say that a five-hundred-plus-page manuscript is at the very least fifty-plus pages too many. Although it often deals with serious issues, chick lit is supposed to be fun and entertaining; it shouldn't weigh more than *War and Peace.* In addition to a clever premise and an equally clever heroine, this book, I soon discovered, had a seriously sagging middle. So I rolled my sleeves up, got out my pencil, and dug in, leaving *delete*s and *X*s in my wake.

I ended up cutting whole scenes and an entire subplot. In some cases I took dialogue that stretched on for twenty pages and whittled it down to five. The author was, understandably, freaked out at first. But once she got to revising, she embraced my way of thinking. (I love it when that happens.) In the end, we managed to lose about seventy-five pages—and gain a stronger book.—*FJ*

Cutting whole characters or storylines is not fun. You've likely put a lot a work into creating that person or plot point. But just because something doesn't work in one book doesn't mean it can't work in another. If you've had to make a tough cut, take comfort in knowing that not only have you strengthened your manuscript by getting rid of excess baggage, but that if you save all the deleted mate-

rial in a fresh document, you might be able to use it somewhere else down the line. All is not lost.

YOU SHOULD PRESS THE DELETE KEY WHEN

※ Something is distracting from the story, instead of adding to it.

※ A story line is making your plot more convoluted than it needs to be.

※ A character is only there because you really, really like her or him but isn't adding anything to the novel as a whole.

When in doubt, ask yourself, *Do I need it? What does it add?*

Letting Go

There isn't a specific amount of hours, days, or weeks you need to spend on your revisions; you just need to make sure you spend enough time to turn your manuscript into a lean, mean publishable machine.

Just as knowing when and what to revise is crucial to this process, knowing when to *stop* tinkering is equally important. If you've done a healthy amount of revising, gotten feedback, revised some more, and then find yourself rewriting the last page over and over and over again, you must take immediate action. Maybe send the manuscript to a friend or critique partner, someone who'll be straight with you, or . . . get ready to send it out into the exciting world of agents and editors (or, more likely, their assistants). We know this might be shocking to hear, but if you don't submit it to anyone, your chances of getting published are seriously diminished. And we'd hate for you to doom your manuscript before it even has a chance.

Thirteen

It's Done! Really! I Promise! Now What?

✳ ✳ ✳

Your manuscript is finished. Revised. Ready to be published.

We know what you're thinking: *What do I do now?*

Now is when you muster up your confidence, patience, and urge to stand in line at the post office and send your manuscript out to the people who can make your dreams of being published come true.

Where Do You Send It?

Who should you send your pride and joy to? You have two options: agent or editor. If you have a specific publisher in mind and you know they accept unsolicited submissions,* feel free to send it to an editor there, but know that your material might sit at the bottom of the slush pile** for a while. Editors and their assistants want nothing more than to be able to get through their slush quickly, as the piles tend to grow and grow and take over corners or chairs or shelves, but their plates are full, and the slush is usually the first thing to suffer.

Which is why it might be better for you to get an agent before you hit up a publisher. Agents are more likely to read unsolicited submissions, first of all. And agents who are looking to sign new writers will get through their slush faster than editors who are overwhelmed and who are, not surprisingly, looking to their agent friends to send them the next big thing.

Publisher or Perish?

You've decided to ignore our advice and go straight to a publisher. (That's the thanks we get for all our hard work?) We'll tell you more reasons why that's not a good idea in the next section, but first we'll help you in your quest.

Only a few publishing houses still accept unsolicited submissions, so do your research before you waste your time and money sending material out to every publisher under the sun. Below are the

---

*An unsolicited submission *is a manuscript or proposal that nobody solicited. Nobody ever asked to see the material, and therefore no editor has allegiance to it.*
**The slush pile *is where all unsolicited submissions go at publishing houses that actually accept unsolicited submissions. Suffice it to say, your proposal often lives under an assistant's desk or on an overcrowded shelf.*

names of some chick lit imprints we know won't recycle your submission or return it to you unopened (because if a publisher says they don't accept unsolicited submissions and you send yours anyway, that's what will happen to it).

Red Dress Ink

Send only a query letter (see pages 170–172) to

Red Dress Ink Submissions
233 Broadway, 10th floor
New York, NY 10279

Avon Trade

If your manuscript straddles the line between chick lit and contemporary romance, you can send your query by e-mail to AvonRomance@harpercollins.com and put *query* in the subject line. You should include a synopsis of no more than five hundred words. Paste it into the body of the e-mail; they don't like attachments (read: They *will not read* your query if you send it as an attachment).

Tor

New to chick lit as of 2005, Tor accepts proposals from unagented authors. You can find exactly what the editors are looking for on Tor's Web site, www.tor.com/torforgechicklit.pdf. Send a proposal with cover letter, two- to three-page synopsis, and the first three chapters to

Tor Editorial Submissions
175 Fifth Avenue, 14th Floor
New York, NY 10010

Making It/Dorchester

Send either a query letter or your synopsis and first three chapters to

Editorial Assistant
Making It/Dorchester Publishing
200 Madison Avenue, Suite 2000
New York, NY 10016

Submissions policies are subject to change, so double-check this information before you send anything out. If you can, find out who the appropriate editor is and address your letter to her. Reference books such as the *Literary Market Place* (LMP) or *Writer's Market* should have relatively up-to-date information. But some things don't change. For example, you should be certain that what you're sending matches what the publisher is looking for. You can do this either by reading books the house has published, looking in the LMP, or looking at the submissions guidelines that can be found on most publishers' Web sites.

If you want your chapters returned to you, include a self-addressed stamped envelope (also known as an SASE). You could also include a postcard addressed to you that the editor can date and drop in the mail so you won't worry your package got lost in transit.

Most publishers take at least a few months to get back to you, so be patient. *Do not* call, e-mail, or send a carrier pigeon to check on your status two weeks after you mailed your package. *Do not* call repeatedly. *Do not* find an editor's e-mail address and send a quick inquiry. If you've been waiting more than a few months and haven't heard a peep, by all means send a follow-up note. But as a general rule, the more you harass an editor, the less likely she is to want to work with you. (Harsh but true. Sorry.)

Your Very Own Jerry Maguire: Your Agent and You

Despite our wise counsel, you might have mixed feelings about getting an agent. On the one hand, you're dying to say, "Can I call you back? My agent's on the phone." On the other . . . don't they take a chunk of your hard-earned cash?

Yes. Yes, they do. Agents generally take 15 percent of what you earn on every book they sell for you. That's 15 percent of your blood, sweat, and tears. So you're probably wondering why you can't just be your own agent and pocket that 15 percent, right? There are reputable publishers who accept unagented submissions; you'll just stick with one of those.

Here's the thing: There are those few publishers who'll look at your proposal, but the majority won't. Editors at Hyperion, Kensington (Strapless), Penguin (Berkley, Dutton, NAL, Plume), Random House (Ballantine, Bantam, Broadway, Crown, Delta, Dial Press, Doubleday, Villard), St. Martin's (Thomas Dunne), Harpercollins (HarperPerennial, Morrow, Regan Books), Simon & Schuster (Atria, Downtown Press, MTV Books, Pocket, Scribner, Simon Spotlight), and Time Warner (5 Spot; Little, Brown; Mysterious Press; Warner Books) are all unreachable unless you have an agent (or unless you know someone who knows someone). So, the most important thing an agent does is get you access. Good agents know which editors are at which houses and what they're looking for. They have a Rolodex filled with contact information. They meet editors for lunch and drinks and see them at book parties and readings. Since they have close, personal relationships with editors, a call from an agent will rescue your manuscript from a trip to the dreaded slush pile and will ensure that it will actually get read this year.

Can *you* do that? Didn't think so.

Agents also negotiate. They get you the best deal you can possibly get. You don't know what the industry standard is, so if you're going it alone, you'll have no idea if what you're being offered is a good deal. As in any business deal, a publisher's first offer is not necessarily its top offer. If you do go straight to a publisher and you get an offer, yes, you should thank your lucky stars (and be proud of your hard work), you should be happy and appreciative, but you should also try to score the best deal possible. Without an agent, you might be shortchanging yourself.

Or, you might be signing away rights you didn't even know existed. Because when you sell a manuscript, there's more to consider than simply how it'll end up in your local bookstore. There are foreign rights and (fingers crossed) dramatic, audio, and first serial rights. (See page 166 for definitions of these terms and more.) Do you want to figure out who to send your book to in the UK? In Italy? In Hollywood? An agent either knows all this or works with someone who does.

You know the good cop, bad cop routine on *Law & Order*? It happens in publishing, too, and trust us, you don't want to be the bad cop. If you want your editor to pick up the phone when you call, then you're better off being the "nice" one. It's an agent's job to pester editors, marketing people, and publicists about plans, reviews, and sales. Perhaps these are issues you want to concern yourself with, but shouldn't you be busy writing?

Agents counsel you, too. They can tell you whether you should sign world rights away, or if you should try selling to foreign territories separately. (Agents generally take 20 percent when they sell your foreign rights—10 percent for them and 10 percent for the international co-agent.) They could help you get a preempt, or if you're lucky enough to have more than one offer, an agent will hold an auction and will help you decide which house to choose.

In addition to all the business they take care of for you, agents can also help you with your writing. They're publishing professionals. They know when a manuscript is a diamond in the rough and can give you advice on how to make it shine. They can turn your humble novel into a hot property.

Most authors we spoke to who were unagented when they signed their first deal wish they had had representation. Melissa Senate certainly does. "I didn't have an agent because I thought, *Hey, I used to work for the company that's buying my book! I don't need an agent! I can negotiate my own contract!* But I was so overjoyed that Red Dress Ink wanted to buy my manuscript that I forgot I was entering into a business relationship and said a gleeful 'yes!' to everything that was offered. Some authors are fine with negotiating on their own behalf, but I'm incapable, so an agent is necessary for me. Lesson: Know what you're signing or hire someone who does!"*

If you get an offer directly from a publisher and really don't want an agent, *please* at least hire a lawyer to negotiate your deal and

---

*I second Melissa's comments. When I signed my deal for Milkrun, I was so relieved to be paying off my Visa bill that I never stopped to wonder if it was the best deal for me. It may have been, but I wish I had had my agent back then.—SM

check out your contract. And not your uncle or roommate-who-happens-to-be-a-lawyer lawyer. A contract lawyer who specializes in publishing.

IMPRESS YOUR AGENT:

PUBLISHING TERMS YOU SHOULD KNOW

Auction: When so many houses want to buy your book that they all bid against each other. The book usually goes to the house that is willing to pay the most.

Audio rights: The right to turn your book into an audio book. If you sell these, that friend of yours who hasn't read a book in years won't have any excuses.

Co-agent: A second agent who works with your agent to sell subsidiary rights. Agents often use co-agents to sell foreign and dramatic rights. Double the fun.

Dramatic rights: The right to turn your book into a movie or TV show (*In Her Shoes*, *See Jane Date*, *Sex and the City*). Break out the popcorn.

Foreign rights: American publishers are only part of the game. You can sell your book to publishers in Germany, Italy, France . . . You can tell everyone you're big in Japan.

Preempt: If a house loves your novel, they may offer you a great deal with the condition that your agent not entertain offers from anyone else.

Serial rights: This is the right to sell excerpts of your novel to magazines. "First serial" goes to the publication with the first exclusive excerpt rights; "second serial" comes next. You know, in case both *Cosmo* and *Redbook* want to print an excerpt.

Subsidiary rights: This umbrella term encompasses foreign, film, audio, and other rights.

World rights: When a publishing house buys the right to publish your book around the globe. Hope you have a passport handy.

How to Find an Agent

How do you actually find this Wonder Woman? You'll need to do some legwork. The key is to identify agents who represent books similar to yours. If you send your manuscript to one who only represents nonfiction, we promise you that agent isn't going to take you on. No, not even if you've included brownies.

You don't have to be a publishing insider to get results. Robyn Harding, author of *The Secret Desires of a Soccer Mom*, found her agent via the submission form on his Web site. "I filled it out, and about two weeks later, he asked for a few chapters. Shortly after that, he requested the whole manuscript, and I signed with him a few weeks later."

But how do you find the agents' names? One way is to flip open books you admire and check out the acknowledgments. Every writer (or at least the nice ones) thanks her agent. You could also head to the bookstore or library and check out *Writer's Market* or *Literary Market Place* for excellent updated listings. And don't forget to study industry hot spots like *Publishers Weekly* magazine or publishersmarketplace.com (where you can sign up for a free e-mail called Deal Lunch) to find out the latest on what books are selling and who's representing them. Another useful source is the Association of Authors' Representatives' Web site (www.aar-online.org), which features an agent database.

Of course, knowing people can't hurt. If you're acquainted with any published writers, ask them for referrals. This only works if you *know* authors, not if you're e-mailing them cold. (Because why would someone you don't know refer you? You could be a serial killer.) If someone agrees to refer you, ask that person to tell the agent to expect your query. That proves that the relationship between the referrer and you is real.

If everyone you know is a hairdresser, chef, or lawyer, consider networking. This might mean joining writers' associations, going to conferences, entering contests judged by reputable editors and agents, or joining writing chat rooms. Networking works. According to Jennifer O'Connell, author of *Bachelorette #1*, "The best thing about being a chick lit author is all the great women you meet. It's such a supportive, fun, funny crowd. The informal network has been the most helpful. We commiserate, laugh, ask questions, and cheer each other on." If you're sharing a laugh, you're one step closer to sharing an agent.

Cara Lockwood (*Pink Slip Party*) thinks belonging to the Romance Writers of America association has been helpful. "Romance is different than chick lit, but I think that it's a good organization in terms of making contacts with other women writers, editors, and agents." There's also a special chick lit chapter of the association.

If you're really lucky, you might hit it off with an editor at a conference. Before one such fateful evening, Laura Caldwell had almost given up shopping around her first novel, *Burning the Map*. "I couldn't get a single person interested in the book. I wrote to every agent in the Western Hemisphere and was met with grand indifference. Then I met my editor at a writer's conference cocktail party.

She was interested in seeing my book. I went back and revised it, and it was published almost two years later.*

It's OK to submit material to more than one agent at a time, but if one of them offers you representation and you're sure you want to accept, let the others know immediately. If other agents take the time to read your proposal or complete manuscript and then find out it's no longer available, they might not be as happy about your good fortune as you are. (Because you've wasted their time, see?)

What Exactly Should You Send?

Once you've made your list of agents, it's time to start pitching. What do agents want? It depends on the agency. You should check each agent's guidelines (either online or in one of those books we mentioned) for specifics. But as a general rule, they want a cover or query letter, a synopsis, a brief author bio, and, in many cases, part of the book. It's a good idea to send a reasonable number of pages to get your style across and the plot moving and to leave it at a point of intrigue. Agents will always request more when they're intrigued. Three chapters is generally the norm, but it's not a rigid rule. When they say "three chapters," they mean the first three. Not chapters 2, 7, and 10. And if you're sending out a query, your manuscript had better be complete. No one wants to get excited about an idea then wait for a year to read it. By the time that year is up, we can pretty much guarantee that person won't be waiting—or interested—anymore.

Some agents will accept queries via e-mail or a Web site (like Robyn Harding's agent), but traditional snail mail submissions are

---

For the record, once Caldwell had an offer from Red Dress Ink, she got herself an agent.

still pretty common (just don't forget that SASE). And no matter whether you're sending a simple query or the whole manuscript (which means you cleared the first hurdle and someone requested your complete novel), presentation counts.

* Your manuscript should be typed, double-spaced, with one-inch margins, and printed on white paper.

* Your type size should be 12 point, and your font should be something basic, like Times New Roman, Courier, or Arial.

* Make sure the pages are numbered and include a header that lists your title and last name.

* Yes, fuchsia is funky, but since you're aiming for an easy reading experience, use black ink. (Sure, this book is printed in teal, but we submitted it in black.)

* Don't justify your right margin—it makes the space between words look uneven.

* Do not staple, glue, or permanently bind the papers in any way. A rubber band or a large binder clip does the trick just fine.

* Do not tie your manuscript in a bow, cover it with confetti, send it as a floppy disk or CD, seal the box so only a machete can open it, or include artwork, cookies, fudge, or anything edible.

Query Letter

Your query should include the date, your contact information (don't forget your phone number and e-mail address), and a brief but thorough synopsis of your novel.

In the opening paragraph, explain why you're writing. You're pitching your book, yes, but did someone refer you? If so, say it here.

Next up, focus on your story. Keep it simple and play up any hooks. Lee Nichols described her first novel, *Tales of a Drama Queen*, as "a coming-of-age-story about a woman who forgot to come of age the first time around" before delving into her brief synopsis. Fun, quirky, hooky. Sold.

You might also explain why your novel is going to sell like hot-cakes. For example, after her brief synopsis, Johanna Edwards described *The Next Big Thing* as "a fast-paced, dialogue-driven novel that tackles two of today's hottest topics: reality television and the battle of the bulge. I think this book will appeal to any woman who has ever struggled with a weight problem as well as fans of reality TV." You need to position the book. Say it's women's fiction. Say it's *Shopaholic* meets *The Shining*. Say it's hen lit. Say whatever you want, but remember to *position* it.*

Now it's time to divulge who you are, and, if it's relevant, why you're qualified to write this book. For example, Edwards noted, "I graduated magna cum laude with a journalism degree from the University of Memphis in 2001, and served as Arts Editor of the campus newspaper for over two years. In 2000, I received a Hearst Journalism Award for Feature Writing, and I've had articles published in local and national magazines. Currently, I produce WYPL's *Book Talk*, a nationally syndicated radio program that features in-studio interviews with both popular and novice authors." No modesty, please. If there's something cool in your background, something that might help your book get publicity, for example, spell it out.

In the last paragraph, play nice. If you've read one of the agent's clients and think your material is similar, say so. It shows that you've

---

* *In my query for* Bras & Broomsticks, *I wrote,* "Bras & Broomsticks *is Harry Potter meets Bridget Jones's little sister." I think that phrase alone sold it.—SM*

put some thought into why you're contacting this person specifically.

By the way, you can also use this model if you're sending directly to a publisher. A query letter is a query letter no matter who you send it to.

CHICK LIT MAD LIBS: USELESS QUERY LETTER

Dear _____ ,
[editor's or agent's name spelled wrong]

Have you ever wondered what it would be like to be _____
[state of exis-
_____, _____ , and completely _____ ? Well, wonder
tence] [state of existence]   [state of existence]
no more. My character, _____ -year-old _____
[number between 23 and 29]   [woman's full
_____ , is in just that situation in my fictional novel, _____ . Women
name]   [title]
everywhere will relate to this story of _____ , _____ , and fashion.
[noun] [noun]

I'm up on all the latest trends, so my novel is overflowing with

mentions of designers like _____ , _____
[expensive clothing designer]   [expensive shoe
_____ , and _____ . I have also attended many writing
designer]   [popular line of makeup]
conferences and have studied with _____
[name of author or editor you had a ten-
_____ , who
minute session with at a writers' conference or whose seminar you attended]
told me my manuscript showed great promise. My friends who have

read _____ tell me it's better than _____ .
[title]   [popular chick lit author or book]
I had so much fun writing _____ and feel _____ that
[title]   [adverb]
my words and my story are meant to be shared with the world.

I'll call you every _____ until we connect.
[day of the week]

Sincerely,

_____
[name]

Synopsis

If you're asked for a synopsis independent of your query letter, keep it short. Two to four pages (double-spaced) maximum. The synopsis should tell the story and introduce the characters in a smooth and engaging way, and it should reflect the tone of your book. Make it fun and easy to read. Try to explain the plot without overburdening it with subplots. You don't have to give away everything here. Just show that the story has a logical, intriguing plot, a character arc, and a resolution.

No pressure or anything, but editors and agents will be looking at your synopsis to see if you can write. So work hard on it.

It Happened to Me

This is from the synopsis I wrote for *As Seen on TV* to help sell my proposal to Red Dress Ink. They published the book in October 2003.—*SM*

As Seen on TV
A novel about lying, living together, and reality television.
By Sarah Mlynowski

"What are you going to do next? Take his name? Become a stay-at-home mom? Buy a bread maker?"

Sunny Langstein knows her big sister isn't thrilled with her decision to pack up her Florida life and move in with her boyfriend, Steve. What modern-day twenty-four-year-old leaves her promising career, stunning apartment, fabulous friends, and perfect underground parking spot with accompanying convertible for . . . a guy?

When the chance to star on the latest reality television show, *Party Girls*, lands at her feet, Sunny can't decide if it's a porthole straight to cheese-town or the chance of a lifetime. True, she might become a national laughingstock and it pays nothing, *but* it's a job, a job in Manhattan. She'll get to be with Steve. And the perks are incredible: a huge clothing allowance, discounts on Manhattan's finest everything, media contacts, and TV experience.

And since she already quit her job, gave up her apartment, and has no other opportunities in sight, she doesn't have much of a plan B.

The only catch: Party Girls don't live with significant others. They don't have boyfriends, period. If anyone finds out about Steve, she'll be pulled off the show faster than Debb Eaton. (Who? Exactly.)

No problem. Pretending to be someone she's not is second nature for Sunny. She already fooled Steve into thinking she's Perfect Girlfriend: always orgasmic, has minty morning breath, cooks gourmet meals, remains good-tempered when he leaves their laundry in the elevator and she spots the woman on the fifth floor wearing her new Juicy Couture sweatpants, and never, ever goes number 2. Ever.

The show's premiere catapults Sunny into a media frenzy of press conferences, tampon endorsements, TV heartthrobs, S&M toys, and truth or dare immunity challenges. It doesn't take long until she loses track of where she ends and her alter ego, Sunny Lang, the Über Single Superstar begins . . .

Spoiler Alert!

When Steve shocks her by proposing, Sunny is infuriated: She can't wear a ring in public! She can't even be seen with him in public! Devastated by her reaction, Steve tells her it's over. Obviously, the girl he moved in with is gone for good.

Sunny decides their breakup is for the best. What's the point of being famous if you're tied down to one guy anyway? Now she can finally let loose. When she ends up in bed with the star of her favorite TV show and then finds out he has a *wife*, she wonders if she made the wrong decision. As her life falls apart around her, she calls on her sister and friends to help her plan a new life—one with less glitter and more substance.

Only after getting herself back on track is she able to win Steve back. She admits that she took him for granted, and he owns up that his proposal was a pathetic attempt to mark his territory. They decide to try living together as a "public" couple for at least a year, and then they'll revisit the getting married issue. If they're ready.

After all, what's the rush?

All Hail the Queen of the Universe: Choosing the Right Agent

Let's say the fabulous happens: An agent is dying to represent you. Then, because you are conscientious and because you are still waiting for your dream agent, you contact the other three agents you sent your proposal to in order to let them know and see if they've had a chance to read it. They have (or they ask for a couple of days, which you give them, and they read it . . .), and they want you, too! What should you do? Meet or at least talk to each of these agents to ensure the best fit. The agent has to get your book, get you, and get your career vision. If they have an agency contract, ask to see it. Ask to speak to references. Ask them what they've sold recently. Make sure you feel comfortable with their demeanor, since this is someone you might be with for the long haul. Your editor might get a new job, or you might get a new editor, but ideally your agent will be around for your entire career.

Emily Giffin (*Something Borrowed*) advises, "You want to click with your agent as much as you want your work to resonate with her—so don't settle for someone simply because she offers you representation." So true. Having a bad agent is much worse than having no agent. One author we know (who prefers to remain anonymous, so we'll call her Jane—of course) discovered too late that her agent shopped her book to only one house, which seriously limited her options—and her advance. Since no other publishers even had a chance to see her manuscript, Jane will never know whether she got the best deal she could. "I signed up with the first agent who wanted to represent me," she admits sheepishly, "mostly because I couldn't believe a literary agent wanted to represent me."

Do you marry a guy just because he proposes? No, you certainly do not. You decide that you want to spend the rest of your life with him. Even though she'd sold her novel, Jane realized that her agent was not The One. "The experience with my first agent helped me figure out exactly what qualities I needed to look for in a new agent. Someone energetic and dynamic, someone nurturing, who would walk me through the early steps of my career, and who genuinely cared about the future of my books." Since divorces are no fun for anyone, learn as much as you can about your potential agent before you agree to anything.

AGENT CHECKLIST

Use the following checklist to assess how well your agent fits with your needs.

☐ Stands behind your book.

☐ Offers constructive comments on your writing.

☐ Can help with your career goals.

☐ Wants to help you develop your career plan.

☐ Doesn't ignore your phone calls and e-mails.

☐ Makes you feel comfortable with the contract or terms.

☐ Has sold other chick lit or women's fiction novels. If she's never heard the term *chick lit*, she's not the right agent for you.

☐ Does not ask you to pay any money up front, ever.

What About the Benjamins?

You're probably wondering what kind of money we're talking about here. Will the sale of your book get you a new pair of shoes, or are we talking a new five-bedroom house with sauna and pool? How does it all work anyway? You sign the deal and they hand over the money?

Here's your best-case scenario:

You write your book. An agent picks it up and sends it out. Within a week, five editors call to say they want it. It goes to auction, and the price climbs up and up and up and . . .

The price of a chick lit novel has been known to surge into the mid–six figures. Hello, beach house. But—and we're serious about this but—life-changing deals like those happen infrequently. Here's a more common financial scenario for a first-timer (give or take a few thousand dollars): the publisher offers $10,000, the agent counters with $15,000, and everyone settles on $12,500. Of course, if more than one publisher wants your book, or if an editor is convinced your book is the next *Bergdorf Blondes*, you could also end up with a two-book deal for a hundred grand. Go you.

Advance? Royalties? Huh?

Maybe you're wondering what, exactly, an advance is. Good question. It's money you get up front, but it's counted against future earnings, or against your royalties. So let's say you get a $10,000 advance for your book, *Girls in Space*. Generally, you'll get half after you sign the contract and half after you deliver your manuscript (because even though you thought it was done, your editor might want you to make more changes). You never have to give that money back, but whether you make more money (also known as earning royalties) depends on how your book sells. If you "earn out," that means you've sold enough copies to cover the advance.

Chances are, you'll be published in trade paperback instead of hardcover or mass market paperback. (Mass markets are the little books that look kind of cheap and typically cost under $7.99.) Your cover price will be roughly $13. Standard royalty rates are 7.5 to 8 percent, so you'll make about a buck per book. If your book ends up selling 30,000 copies, you'll have earned out and will eventually get checks for a total of approximately $20,000.

Royalty rate		Cover price		Copies sold		your advance		your royalty check
	X		X		−		=	

(Who knew? We could have been accountants.) Publishers generally send out royalty checks twice a year. They have to wait for returns to come back from stores to see how many copies were actually sold, so it will probably take at least two years following the publication of your book for all the cash to trickle in.*

And there are always foreign sales . . .

Knocked Down but Not Out: Handling Rejection

Let's say you've been rejected. By agents, by publishers, by the smelly guy at Kinko's. No one wants to take on your book. You briefly consider bungee jumping off a bridge without that elastic rope. What do you do? Do you revise? Do you move on? Is there any hope?

Your first option is to send it out to more agents. You only need one, right? If the agents keep telling you that they love it but you need to fix this or that, then consider doing a rewrite. But, if you've revised and revised and revised, and you've already sent it to everyone, sometimes the best thing to do is move on. Not to another career, but to a new book. If everyone tells you a book is flawed, they might be on to something. Put it in a drawer. Plan to go back to it later, and know that this is not the end of the world. Carole Matthews has those two rejected manuscripts hidden somewhere, but instead of giving up, she took the feedback she got and wrote *Let's Meet on Platform 8*.**

---

*And don't forget: The agent keeps 15 percent. Of everything.
**Even published authors get rejected. I've said no to proposals from my own authors, who then came up with even better ideas that turned into strong proposals and, eventually, published books. —FJ*

Or maybe you're writing the wrong kind of book. Robyn Harding admits that she wrote a historical romance back in her early twenties. "It was a real bodice ripper, which is strange since I'd never read a historical romance novel in my life. I set it in England, where I had never visited at the time, and did absolutely no research. I think I sent it off to Harlequin, because I'd heard it was easy to get published by them. Obviously, they turned me down, but it did make me realize I could actually produce three hundred pages. Whatever happened to it? I hand shredded it and put it in the recycle bin."

Rejection in one form or another happens to everyone. Remember, you only need two people to say yes—an agent to represent you, and an editor to make it happen.

> "Resolve to have a thick skin. Rejection is simply part of the process. It happens to everyone. Many times. When you receive a rejection letter, just imagine J. K. Rowling and how she was turned down by dozens of agents and publishers. Persevere, believe in yourself, and keep doing what you love."
> —Emily Giffin, author of *Something Borrowed*

The End (or Maybe a New Beginning?)

If you've sold your novel, the best news is that you will never again have to write an entire book before getting paid. Really. Unless you want to. Once you have an agent, she can sell your next novel based on a proposal. You write a synopsis and the first three chapters, and if they like it, you're good to go. No more uncertainty. No more fear of spending a year on a project that might not sell. We'd also like to welcome you to the world of bookstore stalking, where not only do all stores have to have copies of your book, but they'd better be displayed face-out.

But whether you've sold your book or not, we want to congratulate you. It's freaking tough to finish an entire book. Be proud. Buy yourself something pretty. Celebrate out on the town. Or step out of your door (you remember "outside" don't you?), take a deep breath, and pat yourself on your (surely cramped) back.

We knew you could do it.

Now get cracking on book two.

Appendix 1

Books That Will Help You. Really.

Here are some books we've found helpful. Some deal with the technical aspects of writing, while others offer some advice about the writing life. But all of them are written by experts who were good enough to share their knowledge with aspiring writers like us—and you.

E. M. Forster, *Aspects of the Novel* (Harvest/HBJ Book, 1956)

John Gardner, *On Becoming a Novelist* (WW Norton & Company, 1999)

Constance Hale, *Sin and Syntax* (Broadway Books, 1999)

Stephen King, *On Writing* (Scribner, 2000)

Anne Lamott, *Bird by Bird* (Anchor Books, 1995)

Betsy Lerner, *The Forest for the Trees* (Riverhead Books, 2001)

David Lodge, *The Art of Fiction* (Penguin Books, 1994)

Raymond Obstfeld, *Novelist's Essential Guide to Crafting Scenes* (Writer's Digest Books, 2000)

Patricia T. O'Conner, *Woe Is I* (Riverhead Books, 2003)

William Strunk Jr. and E. B. White, *The Elements of Style*, 4th ed. (Allyn & Bacon, 2000)

Pat Walsh, *78 Reasons Why Your Book May Never Be Published and 14 Reasons Why It Just Might* (Penguin Books, 2005)

APPENDIX 2

Awesome Authors and Their Published Chick Lit

The women below were kind enough to answer our questions about their writing process and whatever else we felt like asking. If you're not already familiar with these women and their work, check them out next time you're at a bookstore or library or on the Internet. This list has the potential to provide you with endless hours of entertainment.

STACEY BALLIS

Room for Improvement (BERKLEY, 2006)

Sleeping Over (RED DRESS INK, 2005)

Inappropriate Men (RED DRESS INK, 2004)

MEG CABOT

Queen of Babble (MORROW, 2006)

Size 12 Is Not Fat (AVON TRADE, 2006)

Every Boy's Got One (AVON TRADE, 2005)

Boy Meets Girl (AVON TRADE, 2004)

The Boy Next Door (AVON TRADE, 2002)

LAURA CALDWELL

The Night I Got Lucky (RED DRESS INK, 2005)

The Year of Living Famously (RED DRESS INK, 2004)

A Clean Slate (RED DRESS INK, 2003)

Burning the Map (RED DRESS INK, 2002)

LYNDA CURNYN

> *My Inner Brunette* (RED DRESS INK, 2007)
>
> *Killer Summer* (RED DRESS INK, 2005)
>
> *Bombshell* (RED DRESS INK, 2004)
>
> *Engaging Men* (RED DRESS INK, 2003)
>
> *Confessions of an Ex-Girlfriend* (RED DRESS INK, 2002)

SARAH DUNN

> *The Big Love* (LITTLE, BROWN, 2004)

JOHANNA EDWARDS

> *Your Big Break* (BERKLEY TRADE, 2006)
>
> *The Next Big Thing* (BERKLEY TRADE, 2005)

VALERIE FRANKEL

> *Hex and the Single Girl* (AVON TRADE, 2006)
>
> *The Girlfriend Curse* (AVON TRADE, 2005)
>
> *The Not-So-Perfect Man* (AVON TRADE, 2004)
>
> *The Accidental Virgin* (AVON TRADE, 2003)
>
> *Smart vs. Pretty* (AVON TRADE, 2000)

JODY GEHRMAN

> *Control Freaks in Love* (RED DRESS INK, 2006)
>
> *Tart* (RED DRESS INK, 2005)
>
> *Summer in the Land of Skin* (RED DRESS INK, 2004)

EMILY GIFFIN

> *Baby Proof* (ST. MARTIN'S, 2006)
>
> *Something Blue* (ST. MARTIN'S, 2005)
>
> *Something Borrowed* (ST. MARTIN'S, 2004)

KRISTIN GORE

Sammy's Hill (MIRAMAX, 2004)

ROBYN HARDING

The Secret Desires of a Soccer Mom (BALLANTINE, 2006)

The Journal of Mortifying Moments (BALLANTINE, 2004)

KRISTIN HARMEL

How to Sleep with a Movie Star (5 SPOT, 2006)

MARIAN KEYES

Anybody Out There? (MORROW, 2006)

The Other Side of the Story (MORROW, 2004)

Sushi for Beginners (MORROW, 2003)

Angels (MORROW, 2002)

Last Chance Saloon (MORROW, 2001)

Rachel's Holiday (MORROW, 2000)

Lucy Sullivan Is Getting Married (MORROW, 1999)

Watermelon (MORROW, 1998)

SOPHIE KINSELLA

The Undomestic Goddess (DIAL, 2005)

Shopaholic & Sister (DIAL, 2004)

Can You Keep a Secret? (DIAL, 2004)

Shopaholic Ties the Knot (DIAL, 2003)

Shopaholic Takes Manhattan (DIAL, 2002)

Confessions of a Shopaholic (DIAL, 2001)

CAREN LISSNER

Starting from Square Two (RED DRESS INK, 2004)

Carrie Pilby (RED DRESS INK, 2003)

CARA LOCKWOOD

I Did (But I Wouldn't Now) (DOWNTOWN PRESS, 2006)

Dixieland Sushi (DOWNTOWN PRESS, 2005)

Pink Slip Party (DOWNTOWN PRESS, 2004)

I Do (But I Don't) (DOWNTOWN PRESS, 2003)

CAROLE MATTHEWS

Welcome to the Real World (RED DRESS INK, 2006)

More to Life Than This (RED DRESS INK, 2006)

With or Without You (RED DRESS INK, 2005)

The Scent of Scandal (AVON TRADE, 2004)

Let's Meet on Platform 8 (RED DRESS INK, 2004)

The Sweetest Taboo (AVON TRADE, 2004)

A Minor Indiscretion (RED DRESS INK, 2003)

Bare Necessity (AVON TRADE, 2003)

For Better, for Worse (AVON TRADE, 2002)

EMMA MCLAUGHLIN AND NICOLA KRAUS

Citizen Girl (ATRIA, 2004)

The Nanny Diaries (ST. MARTIN'S PRESS, 2002)

LYNN MESSINA

Mim Warner's Lost Her Cool (RED DRESS INK, 2005)

Tallulahland (RED DRESS INK, 2004)

Fashionistas (RED DRESS INK, 2003)

LEE NICHOLS

>*True Lies of a Drama Queen* (RED DRESS INK, 2006)
>
>*Hand-Me-Down* (RED DRESS INK, 2005)
>
>*Tales of a Drama Queen* (RED DRESS INK, 2004)

JENNIFER O'CONNELL

>*Off the Record* (NAL TRADE, 2005)
>
>*Dress Rehearsal* (NAL TRADE, 2004)
>
>*Bachelorette #1* (NAL TRADE, 2003)

ALISON PACE

>*Pug Hill* (BERKLEY, 2006)
>
>*If Andy Warhol Had a Girlfriend* (BERKLEY, 2005)

MELISSA SENATE

>*Love You to Death* (RED DRESS INK, 2007)
>
>*The Breakup Club* (RED DRESS INK, 2006)
>
>*Whose Wedding Is It Anyway?* (RED DRESS INK, 2004)
>
>*The Solomon Sisters Wise Up* (RED DRESS INK, 2003)
>
>*See Jane Date* (RED DRESS INK, 2001)

ALISA VALDES-RODRIGUEZ

>*Make Him Look Good* (ST. MARTIN'S PRESS, 2006)
>
>*Playing with Boys* (ST. MARTIN'S PRESS, 2004)
>
>*The Dirty Girls Social Club* (ST. MARTIN'S, 2003)

INDEX

Acknowledgments

A lot of fantastic people helped make this book happen, either directly or indirectly, so here's a long list of people we'd like to thank:

The generous authors who not only took the time to answer our questions but gave us great material, too.

Laura Dail, for being Laura Dail (definition: supportive, funny, brilliant, tough, sweet, and all around awesome).

Everyone at Quirk, especially Mindy Brown (you were right about those exercises!), Erin Slonaker, Jack Lamplough, Susan Van Horn, and Mike Rogalski (who totally saved the day by finding the fantastic Chuck Gonzalez).

David Goldman, photographer extraordinaire.

SARAH WOULD LIKE TO THANK:

Farrin, for keeping me on track (who knew teamwork could be so much fun?); my excellent editors over the years—Sam Bell, Wendy Loggia, Selina McLemore, and Farrin—for wrangling my words into shape; my many creative writing teachers (especially Peggy Hoffman) for their lessons and encouragement; my forever helpful mother, Elissa Ambrose, for teaching me how to write; my publicist, Gail Brussel, for all her hard work; my friends and family for their fabulousness; and my husband, Todd, for his support, generosity, and for loving me even when I have to work on weekends.

FARRIN WOULD LIKE TO THANK:

Sarah, for procrastinating from writing one gloomy winter afternoon by calling me at work and saying, "I want to write a how-to-write-chick-lit book, and I want you to do it with me"; Valerie Stivers for reminding me that of course I could do it; Emily Chenoweth for reading an early attempt and assuring me it wasn't crap; Margaret Marbury, for taking a chance by hiring me; Selina McLemore and Zareen Jaffery for putting up with me subtly (and maybe not-so-subtly) bouncing ideas off them; and my family for being proud of pretty much anything I do (yes, Dad, the forklift days were especially exciting).